©Copyright Cherie Wagner., 2014. All rights reserved.

ISBN-13: 978-1501014970
ISBN-10: 1501014978

Printed in the United States of America. No part of this book may be used or reproduced in any form or by any means, or stored in a database or retrieval system, without prior written permission from the author. Making copies of any part of this book for any purpose is a violation of United States copyright laws. This workbook is not shareware, and such as, may not be copied and/or distributed for educational use without express written permission from the author.

This book is sold as is, without warranty of any kind, either express or implied, respecting the contents of this book, including but not limited to implied warranties for the book's quality, performance, merchantability, or fitness for any particular purpose. Neither the author nor the dealers or distributors shall be liable to the purchaser or any other person or entity with respect to any liability, loss, or damage caused or alleged to be caused directly or indirectly by this book.

PHOTOGRAPHY
ROBERT JEWETT www.robertjewett.com

All quoted Scripture (unless otherwise noted) is from:
THE HOLY BIBLE, ENGLISH STANDARD VERSION®, ESV® Copyright © 2001
by Crossway Bibles, a division of Good News Publishers
All rights reserved.

DEDICATION

To the lover of my soul, Jesus Christ my King: You have walked me through the pages of this unforgettable journey every step of the way, teaching me, equipping me, and unleashing me. This is my offering to you. Thank you for awakening this sleeper.

To my best friend and better half, Jeremy James: Thank you for your steadfast love and support of all things Neue Thing. Your dedication to this project went above and beyond. I'm so grateful that the Lord saw fit to put you by my side. More than yesterday and less than tomorrow, I love you.

To my sweet friend and sister in Christ, Susan Marie Schnack: Your steadfast pursuit of our Jesus has both blessed and humbled me time and again. Your determination to know and live the Word of God is unparalleled. Nearly every day I spent writing this study, you were in my thoughts and prayers. Thank you for clinging to Jesus like you do.

To my Timothy in this journey, Rachel Dotzler: Your desire to know God's Word and to wade deeper into the waters of your faith in Christ is truly remarkable. Never lose that passion. Never allow the fleeting pleasures of this world to hinder that flame. Thank you for being my guinea pig in this. You have pushed me closer to Jesus along the way.

CONTENTS

ABOUT THE AUTHOR 6
ABOUT THE STUDY 7
A MESSAGE FROM CHERIE 9

WEEK ONE
INTRO TO EPHESIANS 11
- DAY ONE: WHY "ABUNDANCE" IS OUR MIDDLE NAME 12
- DAY TWO: IDENTITY POINT #1: YOU ARE CHOSEN 14
- DAY THREE: IDENTITY POINT #2: YOU ARE ADOPTED 16
- DAY FOUR: IDENTITY POINT #3: YOU ARE FORGIVEN 18
- DAY FIVE: IDENTITY POINT #4: YOU ARE FAVORED 20

WEEK TWO
KNOWING WHO YOU ARE 23
- DAY ONE: IDENTITY POINT #5: YOU ARE UNITED 24
- DAY TWO: IDENTITY POINT #6: YOU ARE PREDESTINED 26
- DAY THREE: IDENTITY POINT #7: YOU ARE SEALED 28
- DAY FOUR: DO YOU LOVE CHRISTIANS? 32
- DAY FIVE: TWO WAYS TO LOVE CHRISTIANS WELL 34

WEEK THREE
A SPIRIT OF WISDOM & REVELATION 37
- DAY ONE: IF YOU ONLY KNEW 38
- DAY TWO: IF YOU ONLY KNEW, PART TWO 40
- DAY THREE: OUR GOD IS GREATER 42
- DAY FOUR: OUR GOD IS SOVEREIGN 44
- DAY FIVE: THE CHURCH: ONE BODY, MANY PARTS 46

WEEK FOUR
THE HONEST TRUTH 49
- DAY ONE: OCEANS OF MERCY 50
- DAY TWO: OUR POSITION IN CHRIST 52
- DAY THREE: WHAT WE CAN EXPECT IN CHRIST 54
- DAY FOUR: FOR BY GRACE 56
- DAY FIVE: THE EVIDENCE OF FAITH 58

WEEK FIVE
WE'VE BEEN BROUGHT NEAR 61
- DAY ONE: THE PRISONER FOR CHRIST 62
- DAY TWO: THE MYSTERY OF THE GOSPEL 66
- DAY THREE: A GENUINE HUMILITY 68
- DAY FOUR: THE TYPE OF CONFIDENCE WE NEED 70
- DAY FIVE: DON'T GIVE UP 72

WEEK SIX
A POWERFUL PRAYER 75
- DAY ONE: TO WALK WORTHY 76
- DAY TWO: THE MODEL FOR UNITY 78
- DAY THREE: THE GOSPEL IN ONE WORD 80
- DAY FOUR: HE GAVE GIFTS 82
- DAY FIVE: WHEN WE SPEAK THE TRUTH IN LOVE 84

WEEK SEVEN
THE CALL TO NEW LIFE 87
- DAY ONE: TWO TRUTHS AND A LIE 88
- DAY TWO: WHEN YOU'RE ANGRY 90
- DAY THREE: HONEST, HARD WORK 92
- DAY FOUR: THE COST OF DESTRUCTIVE SPEECH 94
- DAY FIVE: REPLACING DAMAGING EMOTIONS WITH FORGIVENESS ... 96

WEEK EIGHT
THE GREATEST LOVE 99
- DAY ONE: AN INTOLERANCE FOR TOLERANCE 100
- DAY TWO: FROM DARKNESS TO LIGHT 102
- DAY THREE: AWAKE O SLEEPER 104
- DAY FOUR: A WISE WALK 108
- DAY FIVE: UNDER THE INFLUENCE 112

WEEK NINE
SUBMISSION IS NOT A DIRTY WORD 115
- DAY ONE: THE 1ST COMMANDMENT WITH A PROMISE 116
- DAY TWO: PARENTING 101 118
- DAY THREE: WHEN NO ONE IS WATCHING 120
- DAY FOUR: GOD STILL SEES 122
- DAY FIVE: THE SPIRIT-FILLED BOSS 124

WEEK TEN
ARMOR UP! 127
- DAY ONE: TRUTH & RIGHTEOUSNESS 128
- DAY TWO: PEACE & FAITH 132
- DAY THREE: THE ASSURANCE OF SALVATION 134
- DAY FOUR: PRAYING GOD'S WORD 136
- DAY FIVE: A BOLD PROCLAMATION 138

WEEK ELEVEN
TO FINISH WELL WITH LOVE INCORRUPTIBLE 143

TEACHING OUTLINES ANSWER KEY 144
HANDWRITE THE BOOK OF EPHESIANS 145

ABOUT THE AUTHOR

Cherie Wagner's life-long passion is two-fold: knowing Jesus Christ and making Him known. To play even a minor role in ushering others closer to Him is her greatest joy. Author of *Found On My Knees*, Cherie desires to continue writing Bible studies for women that will encourage them to know and believe God's Word, equip them to live it, and empower them to take it and transform this generation for Jesus Christ. She writes, she speaks, and she teaches God's Word every opportunity that she can.

Cherie and her husband, Jeremy, live in Phoenix, Arizona, where they are both actively involved in the ministries of their church, Central Christian Church. Their only child to date is their rather fluffy, over-sized cat named Roxanne. Born and raised in Chicago and transplanted to the desert of Arizona, Cherie is a city girl at heart with a wild love for the mountains. A coffee connoisseur, a lover of knowledge, and forever a student of God's Word, she loves life and tries to live it to the fullest. Above all, she desires for this to be true of her life:

> *"But I do not account my life of any value nor as precious to myself, if only I may finish my course and the ministry that I received from the Lord Jesus, to testify to the gospel of the grace of God."* ACTS 20:24

Connect with Cherie at **NeueThing.org**

ABOUT THE STUDY

Welcome to *Awake O Sleeper*! Over the next eleven weeks, we are going on an in-depth Bible study journey together through the book of Ephesians, verse by verse and one day at a time. We will study this book until it seeps out of our pores, flows through our lips, and changes and transforms our hearts. I assure you, we'll be better off by the end of this thing than before we started! Are you ready? I'm so glad you're here!

This workbook that you now hold in your hands is meant to be your own personal Bible study tool. By all means, have your Bible right next to you every time you open this book, because the Word will be your guide above all else. This workbook is only meant to aid you in your study. There are a total of eleven teaching sessions and ten weeks of homework. Each week of homework includes five days, and this portion is specifically intended for you! If you can commit to doing your homework each week, I guarantee that you will be blessed because God's Word never goes out and returns void. Any time spent in it will bless you. I promise.

If you are doing this study with a small group, the questions at the end of each day of homework are intended for discussion. I hope you will engage in this part. One thing I have learned throughout the years of Bible studies I've participated in is that women are desperate for genuine, authentic community. This is my invitation to you to go deep with one another. Move past the surface stuff of life and wade deeper into the waters of fellowship. Share your lives with each other. Pray for one another. Study God's Word together. I invite you to circle up around kitchen tables, round tables, coffee shop tables, and any other "table" that will help you foster community with one another. I wish that I could sit at each table with each one of you as you journey through Ephesians, a book that has become so ingrained within the fibers of my being. Know that although I can't be physically present, I have been and will continue to be found on my knees in prayer for you.

Finally, I want to invite you to engage with the book of Ephesians in a few different ways. Some of you are brand-spanking new to Bible study, and I applaud you for signing up. Others of you have been walking with the Lord longer than I have walked the face of this earth, and I am humbled to lead you. On whatever end of the spectrum you might fall, there is much for you to learn through this and much opportunity for you to grow. Here are four different ways you can engage in this Bible study:

1   Come to class and do your homework. I know that many of you despise the word homework and vowed never to return to school once you had completed it. I get it. I've been there. However, let me tell you that although Bible study might begin as a discipline for you and be something that you don't seem to fully enjoy, desire for it and delight in it are just around the corner if you press on through the discipline. Any runner will tell you that this is true. When you first start running, it's hard. You don't necessarily wake up with a desire to hit the pavement. Your body hurts, and your mind gives you every reason to stay in bed. After a few weeks of discipline, though, you begin to see results, and desire is birthed. You find yourself wanting to run each day, and you're sad if you miss a day. It doesn't end with desire, though. If you keep persevering, delight is the final destination. What once was a discipline is now a delight, something that brings you sheer joy. Come to class and do your homework! Desire is just around the corner. Delight awaits you.

2   If you're anything like me, you like a good challenge. So, if you're up for it, I want to invite you to engage in this study on an even deeper level. In addition to coming to class and doing your homework, read through the entire book of Ephesians once a week. Let me tell you that if you do these things, God's Word will plant itself deep within your heart, and you will grow in your understanding of it more and more. I've done this before, not only with the book of Ephesians, but also with other books of the Bible, and this practice has caused me to become so familiar with God's Word. I desire the same for you.

3   Now, we're getting serious. If you want even more out of the next eleven weeks together, I want to invite you to engage further. Come to class, do your homework, read through the book of Ephesians once each week, and handwrite the book of Ephesians in the back of your workbook. This will take some discipline. This will take some time. This will also cause God's Word to come to life within you. Each day of homework begins with a portion of the book of Ephesians that we will study that day. If you choose to engage with this study at this depth, when you begin your homework each day, you'll turn to the back of your workbook, and you'll write out those verses for that day. It will take you ten weeks to do this, but the truth that you pen will stir within you for a lifetime. Have fun with this one!

4   Ok, if you've read this far, you're hungry for more! Here goes. If you want to engage even deeper in this study of Ephesians, and if you want the words of Ephesians to mark you until you take your final breath on this earth, then come to class, do your homework, read through the book of Ephesians once each week, handwrite the book of Ephesians in the back of your workbook, and MEMORIZE the book of Ephesians, in part or in whole. Hear me in this. When we commit God's Word to memory, it transforms our minds. Truth begins to be the first thing in our minds and on our tongues when we face temptation. I'm not suggesting that this will be easy, but it will be so beneficial. Maybe you can memorize the entire book. Maybe you will choose to memorize portions of it. If you're going to go for all six chapters, give yourself six months to do this, one chapter per month. Whatever you can do, do it! It will bless you!

So, which will it be for you? Go ahead and circle the number that you are going to commit yourself to over the next weeks and months ahead. Share this commitment with your small group or the ladies at your table. Now, let's run this race with perseverance. Let's press on toward the prize that God has for us in this. Let's do this thing!

A MESSAGE FROM CHERIE

friends,

I hope it's OK that I call you friends, because that is what you are to me. I might not know you by name, but I imagine that you have come to these pages for more than likely the same reason that I have: to know Jesus more. That makes us friends in my book. That makes us sisters. I pray that this offering of mine will usher you closer to the feet of Jesus and lead you deeper into the waters of His love and grace, just as it has for me.

My first Bible study, *Found On My Knees*, was just as much a labor of love as this one, but it was such a different journey for me. God had graciously walked with me, hand in hand, from brokenness to blessing (the message of *Found On My Knees*) a few years before I ever put one word of that study to paper. *Awake O Sleeper* has been remarkably different. Had I known the places the Lord was going to lead me through this study in advance, I would have backed out before I ever started. Each day that I wrote and studied the book of Ephesians, I was convicted, challenged, and changed. It was an uncomfortable process, but a necessary one. It was a hard work, but a good work. It was a season of pruning, but it has produced much fruit in me. I pray it does the same for you.

Something unique to this study unlike my first is that I wrote it all over the world. From the deserts and mountains of Arizona, to California, to the beautiful northwest cities of Portland and Seattle, to hipster Austin, to humid Houston, to my favorite Chicago, throughout Germany, and even in Thailand, God met me on the pages of Ephesians, and He gave me this message for you, one that has been stirring inside of me for years. More than anything, I want to know God's Word, and I want to make it known. I desire to see the church believe truth and live truth.

In the same way that the inspiration for this study came from so many different places, I understand that you all come to these pages from different places and different walks of life. God meets you exactly where you are. Know this, today. He met me in my fear and complacency, and He took my hand in His as we wrote this together. Without Him, I'm inadequate. Without Him, I'm unable. With Him, there is nothing that is impossible.

Take a deep breath, and prepare to jump in. Paul's letter to the church in Ephesus will encourage you, convict you, inspire you, and propel you into Christ-likeness. Get ready, because once this change in you begins, you'll never want to go back.

Let's aim for Jesus in this!

Cherie Wagner

week one
INTRO TO EPHESIANS

TEACHING OUTLINE

WEEK 1
INTRO TO EPHESIANS

EPHESIANS 1:1-2

1 Even the _____ _____ can be _____ by God's grace. (verse 1a)

2 It is possible to be _____ in a world that is _____ (verse 1b)

3 _____ and _____ can flow from your life even when your world seems to be falling apart. (verse 2)

 If you have committed to write out the book of Ephesians, take a few minutes right now to write Ephesians 1:1-2 in the back of your workbook.

DAY 1
WHY "ABUNDANCE" IS OUR MIDDLE NAME

 "Blessed be the God and Father of our Lord Jesus Christ, who has blessed us in Christ with every spiritual blessing in the heavenly places..." EPHESIANS 1:3

It's amazing to me how much of my life is spent wanting something that I don't have. Think about it—the time, the energy, the focus that is spent on wanting. A new car, a bigger house, a better marriage, deeper friendships, more money, longer vacations, shorter work hours, obedient children, satisfaction and fulfillment, purpose...and the list goes on. I'm not sure there has ever been a day when I wasn't after something that I wanted but lacked.

This is the way of our world today. A constant craving for more adequately depicts the culture in which we are immersed. At the end of the day, the unmet desires create space in our hearts for discontentment and unhappiness. If you were to be honest with yourself, is there something that you are living without right now that is causing you to lose your joy?

I believe we have forgotten the abundance that is our heritage in Christ. In just one short verse of Scripture, Ephesians 1:3 informs us of a very great and precious promise:

God has given us EVERY spiritual blessing.

Not a few, not some, not even several—EVERY. In Christ, there is not one thing that we lack. Abundance is our middle name. In Christ, we have access to "every spiritual blessing in the heavenly places." Meaning? We can have love for our enemies. We can have joy even when our circumstances are anything but joyful. We can know peace during the fierce uncertainties of this life. We can have patience when waiting seems utterly impossible. We can exhibit kindness when the world around us is cruel. We can be characterized by goodness when no one else seems to be doing the right thing. We can possess faith in the face of fear. We can be gentle when others treat us harshly. We can be self-controlled when temptation comes our way.

In Christ, we lack nothing. In Christ, we have no cause or reason for discontentment. In Christ, we have been given more than we need. In Christ, abundance is our middle name.

WEEK ONE

DAY 1
TIME FOR REFLECTION

1. Look up the word *abundance* and write out the definition below.

2. Is there anything in your life right now that is causing you to feel discontentment?

3. Read 2 Corinthians 1:3-5 and reflect on this blessing. Write a prayer of response to these verses.

DAY 2
IDENTITY POINT #1: YOU ARE CHOSEN

 "...even as He chose us in Him before the foundation of the world, that we should be holy and blameless before Him."

EPHESIANS 1:4

Welcome to our second day of Bible study together! Over the next few weeks, you and I will have the opportunity to have a much needed identity crisis. Each one of us will have a choice to either continue allowing the world to define who we are or allow Christ to define who we are. I pray you choose the latter.

Have you ever felt passed by, forgotten, or overlooked? I imagine we all have at one time or another. Every time we have not been chosen seems to engrave on our hearts "rejection," "worthless," and "no good." These words are heavy weights that strip us and leave us hurting and wanting, and we wear them as labels around our necks.

But then, there is Jesus. Before the world came to be, He chose you. He chose me. He selected you. He selected me. He called you by name and said, "Child, you are mine." It is upon this truth that we must begin building our identity.

Many of us have allowed our own mistakes or the mistakes of others to define who we are. No longer! To be chosen signifies a value that is worth mentioning. It's not that there was ever any inherent value within us; rather it is the fact that the One who chose us holds great value. Our value rests in the One to whom we belong. God chose us; therefore, we are His. Because we are His, we are not worthless. We are not the mistakes of our past. We are not our insecurities. We are not our failures. We belong to Him; therefore, He defines who we are. Because we are chosen by Him, we are valued and have great worth. Because we are chosen by Him.

I wonder if there are some of you today who have carried around the heavy weight of rejection for so long that you no longer know where it ends and you begin. It has engulfed you. It has affected nearly every part of your life. Even if someone were to try to love you, you wouldn't allow them to because the past rejection you've endured has taught you to build your walls high and deep. No one is getting in. Rejection has taught you to believe many lies about yourself. You don't trust. You don't love, at least not easily.

Hear this today, friend. When the whole world turns their back on you, *Jesus never will.* When man betrays you, *Jesus never will.* When your friends forget you, *Jesus never will.* When people use, abuse, and discard you, remember: *Jesus never will.* When at every turn you find rejection, Jesus chooses you. He will never leave your side. You are not alone. You have been chosen by a King.

I pray that today is the day that you let down your guard and let Christ in. I pray today is the day that you find freedom. I pray today is the day that your hard heart softens to His touch. I pray today is the day that you embrace the truth that you have been chosen. The work has already been done. He has chosen you. He has extended His hand of grace to you. Reach back and take His hand. Your identity is found in Him and no longer in what has been done to you or said about you. You are chosen.

WEEK ONE

DAY 2
TIME FOR REFLECTION

1. Is there a wound of rejection that you have been carrying with you?

2. Read 2 Thessalonians 2:13 and write it out below. Why are we to give thanks?

3. When this world rejects us, God chooses us. According to Matthew 25:34, what is our inheritance as God's chosen?

DAY 3
IDENTITY POINT #2: YOU ARE ADOPTED

 "In love, He predestined us for adoption through Jesus Christ, according to the purpose of His will, to the praise of His glorious grace, with which He has blessed us in the Beloved." EPHESIANS 1:5-6

Some of our close friends went through the adoption process a few years ago when they added their amazing son to their family. Fast forward to the present, and we find them in the middle of the process again as they are seeking to now add their adorable daughter to their clan through adoption. I think about them and pray for them often in this process, and every time I do, my heart swells with joy. Why? Because I believe the heart of God beats for this very thing…adoption.

Before we were in Christ, we were alienated from fellowship with God. We were separated and far away. We were like orphans. When we come to faith in Jesus, a miraculous event occurs—adoption. He chooses us, welcomes us into His family, loves us as His own child, grafts us in, and now we belong. Ephesians 1:5-6 tells us that before the creation of the world, His love was set on you and me. Before one of your days came to be, He thought of you and said, "I want that one."

I don't know what that does to you, but it wrecks me! Having spent much of my life without a father figure to look up to and having felt somewhat lacking in the "love and comfort" department, this understanding of God's heart for me just overwhelms me. That He would choose me. That He would want me. That He would call me His child. That He would adopt me into His family. I'm undone. There is no greater love that you or I could ever find on this side of heaven.

Perhaps your story differs from mine. You had an incredible earthly father who loved and adored you. Still, being chosen and wanted matters to us all, and it speaks volumes of God's heart and His character to us. The greatest love that we could ever know here on earth—God's love outdoes even that. He set His affections on you and me. He took great delight in us, and He decided in advance that He wanted us to sit at His table.

To know God is to understand this defining characteristic of who He is. He is our adoptive Father. When He could have walked past us and chosen someone who seemed to be more fitting, He stopped, looked down, and lifted us up into His arms. When He could have invested His time and attention on another, He instead called us daughters and sons. And He didn't stop at just giving us His name. No. He covered us in His grace.

What extravagant love. What boundless grace. What abundant favor. And it rests on us because He chose to want us. When the world rejects you, remember who chooses you. When the world walks out on you, remember who invites you in. When the world betrays you, remember who protects you. When the world gives up on you, remember who claims you. In Christ, you are adopted.

WEEK ONE

DAY 3
TIME FOR REFLECTION

1. Today's identity point of adoption adds to yesterday's identity point of being chosen. What is the first thing that comes to mind when you think about adoption?

2. Read Romans 8:14-15. How does being led by the Spirit help you to steer clear of fear?

3. The knowledge that I am chosen by God utterly captures my heart. How does being hand-picked and adopted by God make you feel? What does it teach you about His love? Journal a prayer of response to God.

DAY 4
IDENTITY POINT #3: YOU ARE FORGIVEN

 "In Him we have redemption through His blood, the forgiveness of our trespasses, according to the riches of His grace…" EPHESIANS 1:7

Have you ever owed a debt that you could not pay? It's past the deadline, and maybe you secured an extension, but even that has now expired. The amount owed is far beyond your ability to pay and you are stuck. Trapped. No escape. No options. No hope.

I've been in this position before. Knowing that there was nothing I could do to change, fix, or resolve the situation, I was in bondage to the One I owed. Enslaved to the debt of sin, my life was full of fear and uncertainty and void of hope. I learned how to expect the worst in any given situation. I was a prisoner of my past mistakes and failures, in bondage to the lies that led me into the pit that I was dwelling in, and terrified of the inevitable consequences that awaited me around every corner.

Then I met a man named Jesus. A man full of kindness, generosity, grace, mercy, forgiveness, and love. A man who claimed to have already taken responsibility for the burden of my debt upon Himself so that I could be free. A man who told me of the ransom He paid to release me from the chains of my prison. A man who purchased my freedom when I could not. A man who gave His life so that I could live.

Redemption…

Forgiveness…

This is the identity for all who are in Christ. We are no longer tainted by the stains of our past because we've been covered in His righteousness. We are no longer bound up by our insurmountable debts of sin because He has paid them in full. His redemption of us has ushered in the limitless grace of God upon us. We stand among the redeemed and forgiven as washed clean, made whole, new creations, alive, and free! He paid a debt He did not owe because I owed a debt I could not pay. This is the Gospel. This is the Good News. This is atonement—Jesus in my place. And this is our identity in Christ.

This week, we've already looked at a few identity points that the book of Ephesians gives us: You are chosen, you are adopted, and today, you are forgiven. So, walk in it. Receive it. Live as if you are forgiven because you have been. The world has no authority to write your story or to determine who you are. That is God's job, and He has already determined who you are in Him. You're forgiven, but not just in our limited understanding of forgiveness. You are forgiven according to the riches of God's grace. That, my friends, is extravagance. That is abundance. The author of forgiveness chose to lavish His forgiveness on us. Therefore, we stand clean, righteous, and redeemed before a Holy God. Are you in Christ? Then you are forgiven.

WEEK ONE

DAY 4
TIME FOR REFLECTION

1 What is more difficult for you: extending forgiveness to others or receiving it? Why?

2 Look up the definitions of "redeem" and "forgive" and write them below.

3 Read 1 John 1:9 and write it out below. What is the one condition of forgiveness?

4 What would it look like for you personally to live as if you've been forgiven? What is one thing in particular that you can see yourself doing differently under this mindset?

DAY 5
IDENTITY POINT #4: YOU ARE FAVORED

 "...which He lavished upon us, in all wisdom and insight..."

EPHESIANS 1:8

To be favored is to be the recipient of excessive kindness or unfair partiality. It means that you get what you don't deserve, and you do not get what you do deserve. To be favored is to be the recipient of the blended perfection of mercy and grace. Favored. Did you know that in Christ, you are favored?

I have been loving our study of the book of Ephesians so far as we've looked at our identity in Christ. Just in the first few verses of this book, we are given so many identity points that counter everything that we have heard from the world. Everyone and everything seems to shout at us a different word than what God's Word speaks over us.

Your past will tell you that you are inferior and have been forgotten. God speaks a better Word over you and says, "In me, you are chosen."

Your past will say to you that you are discarded and rejected. God speaks a better Word over you and says, "In me, you are adopted."

Your past will say to you that you are condemned. God speaks a better Word over you and says, "In me, you are forgiven."

Your past will tell you that you are not valued and that you are unimportant. God speaks a better Word over you and says, "In me, you are favored."

Does it ever just blow your mind that in our sinful and broken state, while wandering far from God, He pursues us with His love? While we were still sinners, Christ died for us. We weren't required to clean up our act first. Rather, in our depravity, God invites us in. And He doesn't stop at just inviting us in. He seats us at the place of honor. **Favor.** He showers us with His kindness and lavishes His love on us. **Favor.** He has given us wisdom and understanding when the world is starved for it. **Favor.** In Christ, we have been given all that we need and an abundantly more. **Favor.** This is our heritage. This is our identity. In Christ, we are not who we once were. In Christ, we are not what has been done to us. In Christ, we are not the mistakes of our past. In Christ, we are favored, even though we don't deserve it, even though we haven't earned it, even though we can't afford it. It has been afforded to us. Live in it. Walk in it. Be who you are in Christ.

Chosen.

Adopted.

Forgiven.

Favored.

WEEK ONE

DAY 5
TIME FOR REFLECTION

1. Think about what it means to be favored—to be the recipient of excessive kindness or unfair partiality. Read Psalm 139:13-18. How do these verses reinforce today's identity point?

2. Read Romans 5:8 and write it out below.

3. James 2:1-9 speaks of the sin of partiality or favoritism. What is the difference between being favored by God versus being God's favorite?

week Two
KNOWING WHO YOU ARE: IDENTITY

TEACHING OUTLINE

WEEK 2
KNOWING WHO YOU ARE: IDENTITY

EPHESIANS 1:3-14

Past

1 In Christ, we are W<u>anted</u>. (verses 3-6)

*Married
extrovert
inside
children
sick
old
not*

Present

2 In Christ, we are H<u>ighly Regarded</u>. (verses 7-10)

*forgiven
favored*

Future

3 In Christ, we are O<u>vercomers</u>. (verses 11-14)

*Romans 8:31-39
Rev. 12:7-12
Word of their Testimony*

Live who you are in Christ

 If you have committed to write out the book of Ephesians, take a few minutes right now to write Ephesians 1:3-14 in the back of your workbook.

DAY 1
IDENTITY POINT #5: YOU ARE UNITED

 "...making known to us the mystery of His will, according to His purpose, which He set forth in Christ as a plan for the fullness of time, to unite all things in Him, things in heaven and things on earth." EPHESIANS 1:9-10

I have always been a fan of team sports. Much of my life was spent on a court or ball field of some kind. There is something significant about being a part of something bigger than yourself and working together to reach a goal that you can't reach on your own. As a team, you are united in purpose. You work together. Win or lose, you stand together and fight for one another. You wear the same uniforms. The coach teaches the entire team strategies and plays that will help ensure victory for the whole. The team stands together, united as one.

I pored over these two verses from Ephesians for quite sometime before I was able to see this connection. In Christ, you are united with God. You are on His team. Apart from Christ, you are separated, alienated, and alone, just a free agent, hoping to get picked up by someone. In Christ, God reveals His plan and purposes to you regarding Christ and who He is. You're given the inside information. Apart from Christ, you wander and wonder at the future. You don't know the plan. In Christ, the hope of glory is secured. You have confidence in knowing that you're on the winning team. Apart from Christ, hope is nothing more than a distant dream. You don't know what awaits you on the other side of this life. In Christ, you are united with God.

I don't know about you, but being united with God in Christ thrills me. There is such confidence in knowing that He is on my side, that He fights for me, that He defends me, that He reveals His plans to me—plans that one day, every knee will bow in heaven and on earth, and every tongue will confess that Jesus Christ is Lord!

But I will not be among those who are forced to bend the knee come that day; nor will I stand among those forced to confess that Christ is Lord, because I already do. I have been united with God in Christ. This is my identity. Is it yours?

Chosen.

Adopted.

Forgiven.

Favored.

United.

Remember this, friends. It is God Himself who determines our identity, and this is who He says we are in Christ.

WEEK TWO

DAY 1
TIME FOR REFLECTION

1. The truth that we are united with God if we are in Christ is accompanied by some incredible promises. Read Romans 8:28. What promise has been given to those who have been called according to God's purpose?

   All things work together for good

2. What confidence do you receive in knowing that in Christ, God is on your side and fights for you not against you? Read Romans 8:31 and write it out below.

   If God is for us who can be against us

3. Philippians 2:9-11 gives us a glimpse of what is to come. One day, all of creation will acknowledge Jesus Christ as Lord. If we are in Christ, we will bow among those who love Christ, and we will gladly confess His Lordship. Still, others who have rejected Christ will at that time be forced to bend the knee. Write a prayer below for those you know who have not yet accepted Christ, asking the Lord to soften their hearts and to draw them to Himself.

   Rosemary, Emily () will be soften by God

DAY 2
IDENTITY POINT #6: YOU ARE PREDESTINED

 "In Him we have obtained an inheritance, having been predestined according to the purpose of Him who works all things according to the counsel of His will, so that we, who were the first to hope in Christ, might be to the praise of His glory."

EPHESIANS 1:11-12

We've reached an issue in our study of Ephesians—one that is a point of major contention within the church, theology, and Christianity as a whole—the doctrine of predestination. Essentially, this doctrine teaches that before the creation of the world, God chose those who would by grace through faith be saved. Christianity is torn right down the middle over this one. If God chooses some, does that mean He doesn't choose others? Would God be a loving God if He chose some and not others? These are some of the many questions that arise within this discussion.

While I don't intend to settle this debate today, I love that God's Word speaks to such questions that many of us, including myself, wrestle with. Predestination is actually mentioned prior to these two verses that we are looking at today. Ephesians 1:4b-5 begins the discussion by saying, "In love, He predestined us…". If there is one thing that we all need to embrace no matter which side of the spectrum we fall on, it is this: Predestination is linked to God's love. We cannot separate the two because Christ united them in His Word. "In love, He predestined us…".

Those who would fall on the side of Calvinism would say, "God chooses us." Those on the other end of the spectrum, who would call themselves Armenians, would counter, "No, we choose God." Here's the reality that Scripture teaches us twice here in Ephesians 1:

God chooses us first. We choose God second.

There is choosing happening on both sides, but God initiates the choosing, which only speaks further to His awesome love. He is a Holy God who places His affections on sinful man. The author of Ephesians, the apostle Paul, knew this reality to be true in his own life very well. He was a man who persecuted the first Christians, watching in approval as some were martyred for their faith in Christ, who was then chosen by God on the road to Damascus. He was adamantly opposing God, but God called out to Him. God arrested him. God chose him. And Paul responded to God's call by choosing God back.

I know that this theological debate will not be thoroughly resolved through my words today, but my purpose in addressing it is to highlight a key point of our identity in Christ. If you are in Christ, He chose you to be so. Before the earth was formed, you were on His mind, and His plan for you was determined. There is hope to be found in this truth because it emphasizes God's love, not our good works. Everything God does flows from His love because He is love. We don't need to understand every last implication of how His love works, but we can trust it and rest in it and be made whole by it. In love, He predestined us, and it was and is for His glory, not our own. The fact that we have been chosen if we are in Christ is not to boast on anything that we have done, but rather it is to point to what Christ has done. In Christ, this is your identity. Walk in it.

WEEK TWO

DAY 2
TIME FOR REFLECTION

1. John 6:22-59 tells us of Jesus' claim to be the Bread of Life. As He unpacked this truth to those who were listening to Him teach, He laid an important foundation that ties into our identity point today of being predestined. Read John 6:44. What must happen in order for someone to "come to Jesus?"

   No one can come to Me unless the Father who sent me draws him, and I will raise him up at the last day.

2. Predestination is not only an Ephesians 1 topic. Read Romans 8:29. What does it say?

   For whom He foreknew, He also predestined to be conformed to the image of His Son that He might be the first among many brethren

3. While predestination is difficult to fully understand, God's Word is not silent on this issue. Whenever there are gaps in my understanding of God and His purposes, I always run to Deuteronomy 29:29. Read it and use this verse to journal a prayer of response below, asking the Lord to increase your faith in the areas where you lack understanding.

   If we are to be faithful we need spiritual renewal to hear His word and love Him @ all our ❤. Our responsibility is to obey what we know and not pry into what we do not know

DAY 3
IDENTITY POINT #7: YOU ARE SEALED

 "In Him you also, when you heard the word of truth, the gospel of your salvation, and believed in Him, were sealed with the promised Holy Spirit, who is the guarantee of our inheritance until we acquire possession of it, to the praise of His glory." EPHESIANS 1:13-14

I hope you've all been enjoying this trek through Ephesians. We've been going almost two weeks strong, and we're only in verses 13-14 of chapter one! I love how jam-packed God's Word is with truth and practical application. We need never grow tired or bored of what is found within its pages, because it is life giving and sufficient to meet our every need. Never forget that.

Today's passage is no different. I'm on the edge of my seat for this one (literally, I am sitting on the edge of my chair in my kitchen right now as I type)! These first few weeks of our study through Ephesians, we have been focusing on our identity, a prominent struggle for most in our day, and we've looked directly into the wisdom of God's Word to determine WHO WE ARE IN CHRIST. Today, our identity point is that we are sealed. What does that mean, you ask? Let's dive in!

 The phrase "in Christ" or "in Him" is found frequently in Ephesians, so we must begin by understanding that this is qualifying criteria for the identity points we are studying. Not everyone is sealed. These two verses tell us that those who have heard the Word and have believed the Word have been sealed. This is where we can dispense with the notion that Hell couldn't possibly exist in a world created by a loving God, so therefore all people must go to heaven. That is simply not what God's Word teaches. There are millions of people in this world who have "heard" the message of the gospel. The dividing line is whether or not they have believed it. The book of James takes this even a step further in saying that belief is great, but faith without works is dead. (James 2:17)

I can't help but comment on one particular word in these verses that we are studying today—a word that brings a tremendous amount of hope to the believer—the word "guarantee." Did you catch it in verse 14? Go back and read it again. When you and I come to a saving faith in Jesus Christ, meaning we confess our sins and acknowledge that Jesus Christ is Lord and Savior of our lives, we receive the gift of the Holy Spirit dwelling inside us. His presence in us seals us to God and eliminates the enemy's ability to possess us. The old has gone and passed away. The new has come. We become a new creation.

Of course, there are still times when I wonder and times when I doubt. "Could I have gone too far this time, Lord? Does grace still remain for me? Have I been completely forgiven and washed clean?" Have you ever asked these questions yourself? Verse 14 speaks directly to these doubts and fears by using this key word "guarantee." If we have confessed with our mouths that Jesus is Lord and have believed in our hearts that God raised Him from the dead, according to Romans 10:9, we are saved. Ephesians 1:14 serves as a reminder to us that this salvation is secure by the sealing of the Holy Spirit. If our confession is genuine and our faith authentic, then our inheritance in God's Kingdom is guaranteed.

DO YOU KNOW WHO YOU ARE IN CHRIST? LET EPHESIANS 1:1-14 REMIND YOU AGAIN TODAY.

You are chosen.
Ephesians 1:4

You are adopted.
Ephesians 1:5-6

You are forgiven.
Ephesians 1:7

You are favored.
Ephesians 1:8

You are united.
Ephesians 1:9-10

You are predestined.
Ephesians 1:11-12

You are sealed.
Ephesians 1:13-14

This is your identity in Christ. Embrace it and walk in it.

WEEK TWO

DAY 3
TIME FOR REFLECTION

1. Which one of our seven identity points has most gripped your spirit and captured your heart? Why?

   I am chosen I feel special to God Jesus

2. Being sealed in Christ signifies these four truths: We have complete security in Christ, our salvation is authentic, we now belong to God, and we have been given authority in Christ. Which one of these four truths did you need to be reminded of today and why?

3. In Christ, we have been sealed, which ensures our future inheritance—eternal life with God in Christ. Acts 20:32 tells us that God's Word plays a vital part in our promised future inheritance. What is God's Word able to do?

   Sealed me by Holy Spirit

4. Read 2 Corinthians 1:21-22. The word "guarantee" at the end of verse 22 means "down payment." The Holy Spirit has been given to us as a down payment of the future inheritance that we are to receive in Christ. You have been purchased; you have been bought with a price. What is your response to this awesome truth?

   thankful grateful happy

DAY 4
DO YOU LOVE CHRISTIANS?

 "For this reason, because I have heard of your faith in the Lord Jesus and your love toward all the saints, I do not cease to give thanks for you, remembering you in my prayers,…"

EPHESIANS 1:15-16

It's almost astonishing to me how many times I've heard people say that they don't like Christians. What I find to be even more shocking is when that statement flows from the lips of those who would call themselves Christians. As the saying goes, "They will know we are Christians by our love." Something is terribly wrong with this picture.

The apostle Paul addressed a letter to the church in Ephesus which began with a detailed description of their identity in Christ (Ephesians 1:3-14), a description which we've just spent the last two weeks studying together. After he lays the foundation for who they are in Christ, he begins to speak to some of the qualities that those who are in Christ should possess. Not surprisingly, he starts with love.

Jesus' very own words in Matthew 22:37-40 tell us the importance of love and how much it matters to God. In essence, Jesus tells those who are listening that the most important calling we have on this earth is first, to love God and second, to love people. Paul had such a dramatic conversion experience that it doesn't take him long at all to get on board with what mattered most to Jesus. So, he starts with the necessity of love.

Let's note something of vital importance here before we move forward. Paul isn't praising the Ephesians for simply loving well. He finds reason for great thanksgiving because the Ephesians have been found loving other believers well. We have to get one thing straight here before moving on. God loves His church, and He requires that we, as Christ followers, do the same.

So, do we? Do we love God's people? Do we love His church? Or do we find every reason under the sun to ridicule, criticize, and grow embittered toward "Christians?" I know full well that many "Christians" have run that name through the mud. I know that many "Christians" have used God and His Word as a weapon of abuse. I know that the church hasn't always gotten it right. However, we are called to love other believers with fervency. It was this very love that made front page news to Paul and caused him to find great joy and a reason for thanksgiving, even though he penned the words of this letter to the Ephesians while in chains in a dark prison cell.

When we love other believers well, an unbelieving world finally sees the love that makes us a family, and they will want to be a part of it. When we fail at this calling to love other Christians, we give the world every excuse to continue despising us. If we can't even love each other, how on earth are we going to love those who aren't a part of us?

This matters. It's not a back burner issue. God cares deeply about the care and well-being of His church, and we should, too. So, do we? Do you? Do you love Christians? The more we know WHO WE ARE IN CHRIST, the more we will behave as though WE ARE IN CHRIST. This is our identity. This is our calling. Walk in it.

WEEK TWO

DAY 4
TIME FOR REFLECTION

1. Read Galatians 6:10 and write it out below. What is this verse telling us to do?

    Therefore as we have opportunity let us do good to all especially to those who are of the household of faith —

2. Is it easier for you to love fellow believers or those who are outside of the family of faith? Why?

    No

3. Read 1 Peter 4:8 and write it out below. What does love have the ability to do?

    Above all things have fervent love among yourself for (love) will cover a multitude of sins

DAY 5
TWO WAYS TO LOVE CHRISTIANS WELL

 "I do not cease to give thanks for you, remembering you in my prayers,..." EPHESIANS 1:16

This concept of loving other Christians is so vital and absolutely central to our faith that I felt the need to spend another day on it in our homework. I'm a practical application kind of girl. I love reading and studying God's Word, but what really thrills me is knowing how to put what I have learned into practice. I want to grow, and I want to change. I never want to just have a head stuffed with knowledge. I want to have a heart that has been softened by truth and a life that is full of love.

Therefore, we find ourselves today looking at Ephesians 1:16 again. Paul is in the middle of a very long address to the Ephesians, and what I love about his seemingly endless run-on sentence is that each part is packed full of incredible truth that you and I can apply to our lives today. We've already looked at the necessity of loving other Christians. It's not a negotiable issue. Jesus commands us to be obedient in this. It's the "how" that tends to trip us up. In this one short verse, Paul gives us two practical ways to begin loving other Christians well. Are you ready?

#1—Thank God for other believers. It is truly amazing how an attitude of gratitude can change everything. When we choose to be thankful, no matter our circumstances and no matter the people around us, something inside of us changes. A part of our soul draws closer to the heart of God. In just a few words, Paul sets the example for us in loving other Christians well: "I do not cease to give thanks for you." Have you ever tried it? Giving thanks to God for the Christians in your life—whether you like them or not, whether you agree with them or not, whether you share the exact same theology or not, whether you worship the same way or not—have you ever tried it?

This isn't the only place in Scripture that instructs us to live lives of thanksgiving. Take a moment to look up these three verses and write down a common thread that is woven between them all.

Colossians 3:15 and the peace of God rule in your ♡

Colossians 4:2 continue in prayer being vigilant in it with thanksgiving

Hebrews 12:28 let us have grace by which we may serve God with reverence and godly fear

Start with thankfulness. Before you try to change the entire world in one day and right all wrongs, start here. Cultivate a lifestyle of thanksgiving. Thank God today for the other Christians in your life and watch Him begin to change your heart through your obedience in thanksgiving.

#2—Pray for other believers. Prayer seems to be a lost discipline today in the church. Prayerlessness is a disease that cripples God's people. Prayer is not a spiritual gift that is given to some and not others. Prayer is a calling for each and every believer, and we are all to be found in prayer—daily, hourly, and momentarily. Paul tells us here that while he is choosing to give thanks for them, he also remembers to pray for them. Take a moment to look up Ephesians 6:18. What does this verse tell us to do?

Perhaps you've heard it said before, "Prayer changes things." This is a very true statement, but it might mean something quite different than how we tend to interpret it at first glance. The first time I heard that phrase, I thought, "Great! I'll start praying then." I wanted things to turn out my way, so I figured if I prayed, then they would. The reality that I came to learn is that prayer changes me. The more I pray, the more I change.

If there are Christians in your life that you find difficult to love, start by thanking God for them and begin praying for them on a regular basis. It's very difficult to remain bitter toward someone for whom you're praying. It just is. The more you pray for them, the more God changes your heart toward them. This is the love that Christ calls us to. We tend to complicate things when it comes to faith and add a ton of duty to what God has made pretty simple in His Word. Here in this one verse, it couldn't be any clearer.

#1—Thank God for other believers.

#2—Pray for other believers.

In doing these two things, you are loving other believers well. This is what God calls us to. Let's start walking in love.

WEEK TWO

DAY 5
TIME FOR REFLECTION

1. Would you consider yourself to be a thankful person? Why or why not?

   yes because I am grateful for the kindness shown to me

2. Let's practice thanksgiving today. Is there someone for whom you can thank God for today? Write their names below and a prayer of thanksgiving, thanking God for their presence in your life.

   Anna + (Teacher) — Made me feel welcome + watched, reminded me in case I forgot meeting + potlucks + doctor—

3. Now, let's practice the discipline of prayer. Are there believers in your life whom you know need prayer? Write their names below and journal a prayer today, asking God to bless them with every spiritual blessing in Christ.

Week Three
A SPIRIT OF WISDOM & REVELATION

TEACHING OUTLINE

WEEK 3
A SPIRIT OF WISDOM & REVELATION

EPHESIANS 1:17-18

1. A spirit of wisdom and revelation is the _results_ of a sanctified mind. (verses 17-18a)

   Knowing God
   grasp Spirit truth

   transform mind

   Paul's request

2. A sanctified mind knows _Hope_. (verse 18b)

   riches of glory

   a strong confident expectation in the future

   James 1:5 wisdom

   Hope = 1. of Heaven
   2. Salvation
   3. resurrection
   4. eternal life — Titus 3:4-7

   His calling the riches inheritance

3. Our hope _leads_ us to _assurance_. (verse 18c)

 If you have committed to write out the book of Ephesians, take a few minutes right now to write Ephesians 1:17-18 in the back of your workbook.

DAY 1
IF YOU ONLY KNEW

> *"...and what is the immeasurable greatness of His power toward us who believe, according to the working of His great might..."*
>
> EPHESIANS 1:19

Have you ever found yourself joining a conversation right in the middle of a great story? You feel somewhat lost as you try to keep up with the storyteller and all the details they are sharing. You might be able to piece together some parts, but ultimately you don't have the entire story. This is how we probably feel today in reading Ephesians 1:19. To read this verse on its own isn't going to make much sense because it is part of a much longer thought, or prayer, that Paul is expressing in his letter to the Ephesians.

This is one of the things I have grown to love about studying Scripture—context. It's so important to read and study God's Word in context so that we not only understand what is being said, but also so that we don't misinterpret and misapply these words. We're in the middle of Paul's prayer that he's praying for the church in Ephesus, and in verse 18 he writes this phrase: "that you may know." That short phrase is also applied to verse 19, as he finishes his thought. The desire that Paul is expressing here is that they would know God's power, both collectively and individually.

The unfortunate reality of the state of the church today is that too few know, understand, and believe WHO they are in Christ. Therefore, they live lives somewhat handicapped and frail, when in fact, the church was intended to be the tangible display of God's power here on earth. So few, it seems, actually live in this power, this immeasurably great power. Rather, I find that we tend to try to muster up strength on our own, this "pull up your bootsstraps" mentality. We face life with fists clenched—ready to fight, be brave, fake strong—and all the while we're broken inside. But this was never God's plan.

Take a moment and look up Psalm 103:14. According to this verse, what does God already know about us to be true?

I think sometimes we forget that God knows how weak and frail we are, and that He is in no way surprised by it. He's not expecting us to do this thing called life on our own. That is why He sent His Son, Jesus, to earth, to live a perfect life, to die in our place, and to overcome sin and the grave. Because of this good news, the Gospel of Jesus Christ, God now gives us power to live the lives He's called us to live. He's given us power to know Him, to love Him, and to share Him with others. He's given us power to overcome the bondage of sin and brokenness. We don't need to spend the entirety of our lives bound in shame, guilt, regret, and addiction. He's given us all that we need in Him, and this power that has been given to us is not dependent upon us one bit. This power is at work in and through us according to what? "According to the working of His great might." Since He is the creator of this power, He is also the sustainer of it. It is not up to us to do good or be good enough to keep it or maintain it. If we are in Christ, we have not only been given this power—we can't lose it.

Look back again at verses 18-19. Notice that Paul is not asking God to give these believers His power. Rather, He's asking God to cause them to know that this power has already been given to them. How many of God's blessings have you been given that you live unaware of today? Who does God say you are that you have not yet fully known, understood, or embraced? The truth that God beckons us to today is that we have been given power—immeasurably great power. Do we walk in it? Do we operate in it? Do we know it? Because if you only knew the power that has been given to you, if you only knew the power you have access to, if you only knew the power that is at work within you, your faith could and would move mountains.

WEEK THREE

DAY 1
TIME FOR REFLECTION

1. Jesus' last recorded words in Scripture are found in Acts 1:7-8, right before He ascended back into Heaven. Write out these verses below. What did Jesus promise His disciples they would receive?

   And He said to them It is not for you to know times or seasons which the Father has put in His own authority. But you will receive power when the Holy Spirit has come upon you. + You will be witnesses to Me in Jerusalem and in all Judea + Samaria and to the end of the earth.

   Receive power
   Will be witnesses.

2. Knowing that you have been given power in Christ upon conversion, what specific task or calling do you now feel empowered to accomplish or step into in Christ?

   Witnesses

3. Colossians 1:29 speaks further to this power that we've been given by using the word "energy." In what ways do you feel weak or lacking in energy? How does this verse speak encouragement to your situation?

   I strive + labor according to His working which works in me mighty.

DAY 2
IF YOU ONLY KNEW—PART TWO

 "...that He worked in Christ when He raised Him from the dead and seated Him at His right hand in the heavenly places..." EPHESIANS 1:20

Just the other day, I found myself discussing internet speed with a friend of mine. She was getting cable television installed at her house, and I was asking her how much she paid per month for her cable and internet combined. I quickly learned that she was paying much less than we were, and I remembered that when we signed up for internet service, my husband wanted the highest speed internet that they offered, which was also the most expensive. I proceeded to tell my friend how I didn't really think it made much of a difference, but seeing as my husband was the one to use it most, I didn't argue. It wasn't more than a few minutes later that my friend needed to search for something online, and we were both shocked at how slow her internet speed was. And then two things dawned on me: first, my husband is right much, or even most, of the time, and second, your power source determines your speed.

We'll spend the next few days finishing up Paul's thought in his prayer for the Ephesians. Today we find him further explaining the power that we studied yesterday. We have been given power as believers, whether we live aware of it or not. Just in case you aren't convinced yet of this power that God has given us access to in Christ, Paul defines this power in further detail for us today. If you were tempted to believe that "this power" is some sort of superhuman strength, something mystical, or even superstitious, you can toss those theories out the window right now because God makes it very clear who the source of this power is and what kind of power it is. *Holy Spirit*

Even if you haven't retained a single word yet today, DON'T MISS THIS: The very same power that God Himself exerted when He raised Jesus from the dead and when He lifted Him by ascension back into Heaven is THE SAME power that He gives to every believer.

He makes this abundantly clear here. You don't need to be a Greek or Hebrew scholar to see this truth in Ephesians 1:20. You don't need to do a word search to determine if the same word for power is being used. Not in this case. Why? Because this is exactly what it says here in Ephesians 1:19-20—"THE SAME POWER."

So, what does this mean for us today? It means that everything we have studied together so far is true. It means that we are capable of being WHO God says we are in Christ. It means that life transformation and heart change are possible. It means that you don't always have to be the way you once were. It means that there is nothing too difficult for God, and it means that we can do ALL THINGS through Christ who strengthens (or empowers) us (Philippians 4:13). I obviously do not know what kind of power it would take to raise someone from the dead, but I imagine it was a lot. I don't know how much power is needed to lift Jesus by ascension back to glory so that He could assume His rightful place next to God, but I would think it was a lot. To be honest, I cannot imagine anything more difficult to accomplish than raising Christ from the dead or causing Him to ascend into heaven, but the beauty of it all is that THIS VERY POWER is at work within us as believers.

This power, when used, is a dangerous and powerful weapon against the enemy. The truth that God is calling us to walk in today is not only knowing and believing that we've been given power, but that this power is supernatural, equipping and enabling us to do any and every thing that God would ask us to do. If we only knew the power that we have access to, if we only knew all that we could accomplish for the Kingdom with this power, we would live lives of freedom. We would be ushering others to that same freedom. We have been empowered with God's divine power. Embrace it. Hold fast to it. Use it. Walk in it.

WEEK THREE

DAY 2
TIME FOR REFLECTION

1. If you're anything like me, you desperately want this power to be realized in your own life, but at the same time, you have a hard time understanding what exactly this would look like. Read Acts 4:32-35. What effect did this "power" have on this specific situation?

   Shared
   unselfish

   willing to give
   not his own—

2. What effect could this power have on your situation with non-believers in your life?

   They all believed the same

3. The power that we've been given in Christ enables us to overcome, to conquer the enemy, and to walk in freedom from temptation and sin. Read Revelation 12:7-11. Two things gave them power to overcome the enemy in verse 11. What were they?

   blood of the Lamb
   by the word
   of their testimony
   they did not love
   their lives to the death.

   The Lamb overcomes because of His

   fall of satan

   The Lamb Power of the word

DAY 3
OUR GOD IS GREATER

 "...far above all rule and authority and power and dominion, and above every name that is named, not only in this age but also in the one to come." EPHESIANS 1:21

After 168 words (Ephesians 1:15-21), Paul finally finishes his sentence. Don't get me wrong, because I was in no rush for him to finish. Each phrase has been jam-packed with rich truth, but let's just say that his run-on sentences would never make it onto Twitter with its 140 character (not word) limit. The reality is that Paul had much to say to this group of believers whom he loved, and he had one letter in which to say it. Therefore, he held nothing back, but he also didn't waste a single word.

Just this morning, I found myself in a conversation about the importance of words and the necessity of the lack thereof at times. You and I could perhaps learn much from Paul in this: Don't waste your words, but make sure that the "much" that you have to say benefits those who hear it. Every word that was penned by Paul's hand in this letter to the church in Ephesus was purposeful, helpful, and full of truth. Allow this to be a lesson learned for us all today. Our words should follow suit.

Ephesians 1:21 is the first of three verses that will speak of Christ's position and authority. In the event that they had forgotten the deity or divinity of Jesus Christ, Paul reminds them here in this verse. Severe persecution of the first Christians had already begun, and Paul was a first-hand witness to that, being that he wrote this letter from prison, while in chains. Not only was persecution a threat to this group of believers, but in addition to that, so was false teaching. Even some of the Jews of this time had rejected Jesus Christ as the promised Messiah, so Paul reinforces the truth of WHO Christ is.

Take a moment and look up Matthew 28:18, Philippians 2:9, and Colossians 1:16. What do these three verses tell us about Jesus?

Jesus Christ was not merely a good man, not only a prophet, not simply one of the heavenly hosts, and not even just the Son of God. Jesus Christ IS God. Therefore, His seat is in equal position to that of the Father, at His right hand. He remains ABOVE all rule and authority, both here on earth and in the heavenly realms. There is none greater, none stronger, none more powerful, and none like Him. And His name...

Jesus.

His name is above all other names. There wasn't, isn't, nor will there ever be a name greater than Jesus. At the sound of His name, the enemy flees. At the sound of His name, the lost are saved. At the sound of His name, the prisoner is set free. At the sound of His name, every fear is displaced. At the sound of His name, the hopeless find hope. This is our God. And our God is greater.

Jesus is greater than your circumstance.

Jesus is greater than your fear.

Jesus is greater than your heartache.

Jesus is greater than your disease.

Jesus is greater than your doubt.

There is none greater than our God. Many poor substitutes have tried to dethrone our God, but know this:

They never will. Because there is none greater than our God.

WEEK THREE

DAY 3
TIME FOR REFLECTION

1. In your life, what competes for your greatest affections? Who or what tries to be first place?

   TV
   To be in control

2. I have always loved the book of John, and I've always pointed people in its direction who are new to the Bible because it is a great place to start. Read John 1:1-5. The phrase "the Word" is referring to Jesus Christ. If these verses are true, what do they say about our God? About Jesus?

   We can trust Him with our lives
   He is the Creative Word and the living Word who reveals the Father to us.

3. As much as I love the book of John (and the entire Bible, for that matter), my favorite book in Scripture would have to be Hebrews. I'm not sure you're supposed to have a favorite book, but I do, and there it is. Hebrews 1:1-4 talks about Christ's supremacy over all things, even the heavenly beings. Jesus, who is God, is even greater than the angels, and this great God cares deeply about the details of your circumstances. Write a prayer of response to God, thanking Him for being greater than any and every false substitute.

   Dear Holy Jesus thank you for being greater than any others
   for being than my circumstances
   greater than my fear
   greater than my ♡ ache
   greater than my disease
   greater than my doubt
   there is none greater than you
   there will never be because there is none greater than you.

DAY 4
OUR GOD IS SOVEREIGN

 "And He put all things under His feet and gave Him as head over all things to the church…"

EPHESIANS 1:22

One of the attributes of God that I love most is His sovereignty. He holds supreme power and authority and is in control over all things. Maybe I love this about Him so much because I have struggled my whole life with the issue of control and wanting to be in control of everything, only to learn the hard way each time that things in general tend to be better off when I am not in control of them. The more I try to assume control and authority over the details of my life, the more I experience disappointment and pain. Why? Because I was never intended to be in control of my life. Why? Because God's way was, is, and always will be far better than my own.

I wonder if you find yourself nodding your head as you read my above confession, understanding the struggle and wrestling with the tension. We have a very hard time with things like surrender, submission, and humility because we want to be in control. We want to be calling the shots, especially when it pertains to our own lives. This is usually where faith gets tricky because God asks us to deny ourselves, to take up our crosses daily, and to follow Him (Luke 9:23). We, however, like to write out the blueprints for our lives, hand them to God, and ask Him to place His stamp of approval on them. However, that's just not how He works.

Take a moment and look up Psalm 8:6. What similarity do you see in this verse and Ephesians 1:22?

Ephesians 1:22 and Psalm 8:6 are telling us that God chose to exalt Jesus Christ over everything. I usually like the extreme black and white statements in Scripture because I tend to be somewhat extreme myself. When both verses use the phrase "all things," I assume that God means "all things." Therefore, you and I can conclude that not just some things or even most things have been placed under Christ's authority, but ALL THINGS have. That includes the past, the present, and the future. That includes you, me, and all of our plans for our lives. That includes every figure of authority here on this earth. ALL THINGS have been placed under the authority of Jesus Christ. He is in control. He is sovereign over all. There is nothing that is above Him in any way.

I find a tremendous amount of hope in this truth. He is never surprised or taken off guard. He is never threatened or overthrown. Remember what we studied just a few verses ago in Ephesians 1:20? Jesus is seated. He is not pacing back and forth in the heavens, awaiting the decisions we make and anxiously responding to them. No. He rules over all of creation seated. The One who spoke the universe into existence rules over it with His feet up. Not stressed. Not worried. Not anxious. Not wondering.

Sovereign.

Therefore, you and I can let go. Our tightly clenched fists that carry the heavy weight of our problems, fears, and concerns can be opened up to the God who is in control of all things, including the very things that cause our lives to seem out of control. He knows. He is present. He cares. He sees. So loosen that grip on all that you exhaust yourself trying to control, and allow the One who is in control to hold it and take care of it instead. Why? Because our God is sovereign.

WEEK THREE

DAY 4
TIME FOR REFLECTION

1. I would venture to say that most of us love that God is sovereign. The difficulty we come across, however, is when God's plans for our lives differ from our own. Read Isaiah 55:8-9 and write them out below.

   God's way is the best give it all to Jesus He turns your sorrow into joy

2. What principle can we take away from Isaiah 55:8-9, and how can these verses change the way we live our lives?

   Trust God - His ways are beyond our comprehension. But be sure He is accomplishing His purpose in His time

3. Read 1 Corinthians 15:27. What has been placed under God's feet?

   All Things

4. Journal a prayer of response, thanking God that He is sovereign and in control of all things.

   I am grateful to God that He is sovereign & in control of everything

DAY 5
THE CHURCH: ONE BODY, MANY PARTS

 "...which is His body, the fullness of Him who fills all in all."

EPHESIANS 1:23

Have you ever wanted to be good at something that you just weren't good at? When I was a little girl, I wanted to be an Olympic gymnast more than anything. I remember watching the girls perform with such grace and ease thinking, "That will be me someday." I was eight years old. This was my dream. Don't judge and try not to laugh. Reality came crashing down on me, though, when I realized that gymnastics was more than likely never going to be my forte. At the age of eight, I was bigger than most of the gymnasts in the games who were twice my age, and I was growing at a rapid rate. I was never going to be small or petite. I would never fit that mold. I just wasn't built that way. Not to say that I couldn't be good at gymnastics, but my gifts rested in other areas. And I had to learn that this was OK.

You and I both can smile at our childhood dreams and maybe even laugh, but this struggle more often than not continues throughout adulthood. If we are in Christ, God has gifted us with spiritual gifts, supernatural empowerment to do what God created us to do to bless and further His Kingdom here on earth. The problem is that we always seem to want the gifts that we don't have. Certain gifts can appear to receive more press and spotlight, while others seem to go unnoticed, and it is in this wanting and coveting of what we don't have that we forget we are a part of one body and that each and every part matters.

Paul is wrapping up his long, prayerful thought here in Ephesians 1:23 with a reference to the church, but he uses the phrase "His body." After Christ's ascension, the apostles were left with the responsibility of spreading the Gospel. As it spread, more were added to the fold of disciples. This group became the first church. The body of Christ is a metaphor for God's redeemed people, used exclusively in the New Testament of the church. Here in Ephesians, we are told that all things have been placed under the authority of Christ, including the church, and that the fullness of who He is resides in the body, the church. Because this is the order that God set up and because the fullness of Him is in the body of Christ, we as the church have been filled. Is this making sense yet?

This truth speaks further to our identity in Christ. If we are in Christ, we have been filled with the fullness of Christ. If we are the body of Christ, have we assumed our individual roles? We are part of the whole, a piece of a greater picture: One body, many parts. We can't all be eyes, because if we were, who would be the ears? We can't all be hands, because who would be the feet? Do you know your role within the body, and are you using the gifts that God has given you to fulfill that role? You're not lacking anything that you need to function in the role that God has given you. He created you with intention and on purpose, and He equipped you for His purposes. He gifted you with abilities that will further His Kingdom here on earth, and He waits for you to take your place.

There is one body, but there are many parts. The most beautiful picture of the body of Christ is one in which each member ceases striving to be what they are not and rather embraces who they ARE in Christ. That is a healthy body. That is the body of Christ that He's called us to be.

WEEK THREE

DAY 5
TIME FOR REFLECTION

1. In 1 Corinthians 12:7, we are given a very great and important promise as believers in Christ. What is it? Write the verse below.

   But the manifestation of the Spirit is given to each one for mutual profit for all so that we can serve Christ + His church

2. Do you know what your spiritual gift is? If so, what is it, and are you using it for "the common good" of the church?

   Before my 2 strokes
   Helper - worker & Teacher & organized gift together - participate

3. I love that in Christ, we have been filled with the fullness of Him. Therefore, there is no lack, no need, and no void that Christ cannot and will not fill. Read John 1:16 and write it below. Then, look up the word grace and write its definition below.

   And of His fullness we have all received and grace for grace

   He came with grace and truth — not law + judgement

4. What is your response to the truth that in Christ, YOU have been filled with the fullness of Christ? Yes-
   accept it with true humbness —

week four
THE HONEST TRUTH

Truth supplies lies

TEACHING OUTLINE

Eph. 2:8

Pst. 14:1-3

WEEK 4
THE HONEST TRUTH

EPHESIANS 2:1-3

1. Sometimes, we need a sobering __Reminder__ of what we have been __Redeemed__ from. (verse 1)

2. Before Christ, we were followers of this __world__. (verse 2a)   *Proverbs 6:16-19*   "7 Things God Hates"
   1. arrogant verse humility phil 2:3
   2. lies of the tongue
   3. shed blood murder —
   4. 16 wicked planning at the expense of others   Heb 10:24
   5. feet that run to evil the wicked is slow hiding   James 1:19-21
   6. lies a false witness. I swear to tell the whole truth
   7. cause trouble in the family - matter   1 Pet 3:8-12

3. Before Christ, we were followers of the __world__. (verse 2b)

   John 12:31
        14:30
        14:11

   Deuteronomy 1:26

4. Before Christ, we were __Children of Wrath__ *darkness*. (verse 3)

> If you have committed to write out the book of Ephesians, take a few minutes right now to write Ephesians 2:1-3 in the back of your workbook.

DAY 1
OCEANS OF MERCY

> *"But God, being rich in mercy, because of the great love with which He loved us, even when we were dead in our trespasses, made us alive together with Christ—by grace you have been saved..."*
>
> EPHESIANS 2:4-5

Who is excited that we have finally made it to Ephesians chapter two? Three weeks of Bible study, homework, and hard work are under our belts, and although it took us quite a while to get through only one chapter, we have laid a sturdy foundation to build upon. Amen? To those of you who are on your very first journey through Scripture, I am so proud of you! To the veterans of the faith, I am so honored to walk alongside you. To all, I am thrilled to be on this verse-by-verse trek through the book of Ephesians with you. Get ready to whet your appetite even more. Today, we dive head first into chapter two!

As we learned in "The Honest Truth" of Ephesians 2:1-3, Paul held nothing back in painting a brutally honest picture of what our lives look like apart from Christ. There's no pretty way of looking at it. Life before or apart from Christ is ugly, bleak, and depressing, which makes today's portion of Scripture that much sweeter.

I love the word mercy. Just say it, out loud. Mercy. It embodies the idea of not getting what we do deserve, the lifting of the penalty, the removal of the due sentence. After having looked at Ephesians 2:1-3 in depth, we should be fairly certain of what we deserve based on our lives before Christ. Death. That's it. The wages of sin is death, and when we were in sin, we were dead in it, lost, and separated from Christ. "But God" (Ephesians 2:4)...what an incredibly beautiful two words to start us off today. "But God..."

Something we must come to understand when we come to faith in Christ is the richness of His mercy and the greatness of His love. Too often, I've heard people tell me that although they fully believe in God's mercy and love toward others, they simply cannot imagine that God would extend it toward them. In their minds, they have gone too far. They can't possibly believe that God's mercy could or would cover their sin. Even if they don't actually articulate this, their lives are characterized by this belief. They won't darken the doorstep of a church. They refuse to get involved in Christian community. They fear embracing accountability. They won't receive God's mercy. They remain in the pit of guilt and shame.

Let me tell you something about the mercy of God. It's an ocean. It's wider and deeper than the eye can see or the mind can comprehend. It's greater than the heart could long for it to be. Do you know what makes it even better, this mercy and love that brings us into salvation? It rescued us while we were still sinners. That is a good God. That is a loving Savior. That is a faithful Father. That is my Jesus.

When we were dead in our sin, Christ made us alive through His power. This power that brings life from death within us is the same power that energizes and enables every aspect of Christian living. Therefore, although difficult at times, living a Christian life according to the standards and principles of God's Holy Word is possible, even in a culture that rejects it. Take a moment and read Romans 6:11-14. What encouragement do you receive from these verses as you seek to maintain a close walk with Jesus?

Oceans of mercy and waves of grace wash over us as we receive God's invitation of love. The stains of our pasts are made clean, the guilt and shame is removed, and the burdens of our foolish choices are lifted in the oceans of His mercy, beneath the waves of His grace. And He invites you in. Stop wading in the shallow waters. Go deeper. Let His mercy and love overwhelm you and pull you into the depths of His embrace.

WEEK FOUR

DAY 1
TIME FOR REFLECTION

1. One of my favorite passages in Scripture is tucked away in the Old Testament in Lamentations 3. The prophet Jeremiah is detailing the abundant reasons for his grief as he laments over the state of the nation of Israel, hence the title "Lamentations." The entire book is filled with his tears that he translated into words, but then he gets to chapter three, verses 21-24. He says that hope comes when he remembers the Lord's mercy. God gives us the promise here that His mercies will be new every morning. Write out verse 22. If this is true, what is your response to such a gift?   *Thankfulness*

   The faithful love of the Lord never ends
   His mercies never cease

2. 1 Peter 1:3 also refers to God's great mercy. Write this verse out below.

   Blessed be the God & father of our Lord Jesus Christ who according to His abundant mercy has begotten us again to a living hope by the resurrection of Jesus Christ from the dead

3. I pray that by this point, God's mercy is no longer a distant hope, but rather a near and experienced reality in your life. Write the definition of mercy below. How and why are you grateful for God's mercy in your life?

   because his mercy never fails
   & I can call on him any time

DAY 2
OUR POSITION IN CHRIST

 "...and raised us up with Him and seated us with Him in the heavenly places in Christ Jesus,"

EPHESIANS 2:6

I wonder if you're like me at all in this: I love how God's Word is alive and active, sharper than a double-edged sword (Hebrews 4:12). You too? His Word never fails, and it always proves true. When I seek God with all my heart, I find Him (Jeremiah 29:13)...always. I never need to wonder if God will be present when I search out His Word. I never need to guess if His presence will be found when I pursue Him. Every time, He will be found. Every time.

Therefore, as I look into Ephesians 2:6 today and the promises that are found within, I need not wonder if these promises are true. I also don't need to wait for them to come to fruition. They already have. Look at the verb tense for both "raised" and "seated"—past tense verbs meaning that both of these promised things are immediate and direct results of our salvation. At the moment of our conversion, we were raised up from the pits in which we once dwelled, and we were seated with Him, our Father in Heaven.

This should DO something to your soul! This should shake your insides and rock your world. This should cause your heart to flip-flop, all in a good way. We, the lowly sinners and the undeserving, have been positioned next to God in Christ and been found worthy recipients of His mercy and grace. Not only do we enjoy the benefits of forgiveness and the joys of being dead to sin and alive in Christ, but we also share in Christ's exaltation because just as He was raised from the dead, we, too, have been raised from the death that our sin had us bound up in and been made alive in Christ.

Take a moment and read Colossians 2:12. Through what have we been raised in Him? And if we have been raised from death to life, do our lives display this incredible hope? Are you a tangible expression of this grace to the world around you, this grace that has raised and seated you?

Our position matters because it should determine our activity. Knowing that we are seated with God in Christ should cause our future to be drastically altered for His glory. It should challenge us to live lives worthy of our calling, lives that reflect our position in Christ. It should determine our course. It should transform and renew our minds and alter our decision making. So, does it? Do our lives reflect the nearness of God and His presence that we experience on a daily and momentary basis? Do people taste and see that the Lord is good when they interact with us? They should.

We sit next to God. Let that sink in for a moment. The God who is Holy and dwells in unapproachable light that can not even look upon sin, allows us to be seated next to Him in Christ. That is our position in Christ. We have immediate access to Him at all times because of our position in Christ. So, do we take advantage of that access and call on His name, living lives that are in constant desperation for more of Christ? Or do we live as if we could survive much of life without Him? Does a world that is lost without Christ know the hope that we have in Christ based on how we live out our faith? Do they see it in us? Or do we push them further away?

I think we need a reminder today of our position in Christ. We have been raised and seated with Christ in the heavenly places, the supernatural realm where God reigns. Why should this reality thrill us? Because this is where our blessings are found if we are in Christ (Ephesians 1:3); this is where our future inheritance is if we are in Christ (1 Peter 1:4); this is where our affections should be (Colossians 3:1-3); and ultimately, this is where we should enjoy fellowship with the Lord.

So, do we? Do we know, understand, and believe our position in Christ? We've looked at and studied in depth our position prior to Christ, and now we embrace the hope we have been given in Christ.

We have been raised.
We have been seated.

Allow these truths to arrest your soul, to captivate your heart, to renew your mind, and to change your future. You are His, my friends. Your paths are His. Your plans and purposes are His. And your position is in Him.

WEEK FOUR

Jesus

1. In Christ, you are no longer who you once were. What a beautiful thing that is, amen? How has your position in Christ determined or changed your activity? In what ways does your life before Christ look different from your life in Christ?

2. There is a world watching us and determining what they believe to be true about Jesus based solely on what they see in us. What type of responsibility comes along with our position in Christ?

   My responsibility to tell my unsaved friends about Jesus — my actions should reflect Christ

3. Read Romans 6:4 and write it out below. What would it look like for you today to "walk in newness of life?"

   Therefore we were buried c Him by baptism into death that just as Christ was raised from the dead by the glory of the Father, even so we also should walk in newness of life

DAY 3
WHAT WE CAN EXPECT IN CHRIST

 "...so that in the coming ages He might show the immeasurable riches of His grace in kindness toward us in Christ Jesus." EPHESIANS 2:7

Do you have favorite Bible study memories? You know, those times that marked you forever in your study of God's Word? Those moments that froze in time, and when you recall them, it seems as if it were just yesterday that it happened? I have those moments. I have those memories, and I love revisiting them because they remind me of the places I've been with the Lord and the times of refreshing I've had in His presence.

One moment in particular that I want to share with you happened to me years ago when I was in my first women's Bible study. I was one of the youngest ladies in the room, sitting among some incredible women of faith, excited to sit at their feet and glean wisdom from their lives. The first week of the study, the leader addressed us all with one simple challenge: to expect God. Short, sweet, and simple. When we open God's Word, expect to meet with Him there. When we approach the throne of grace in prayer, expect God to be there and to hear you. Expect God. She had us open our Bibles to the very first page, the one that boasts the title "The Holy Bible," and she had us write on it, "I expect you, Jesus." It would serve as a gentle reminder to each one of us every time we opened His Word. Let us all adopt this practice together today and every day moving forward in our study of God's Word: "I expect you, Jesus."

Upon this foundation, we begin our study together today of Ephesians 2:7. Many of God's promises to us in Scripture have already been realized and received. We looked at this yesterday in Ephesians 2:6. Still, there are other promises given to us in His Word that we wait for in eager anticipation and expectation. This is one of those promises. Part of the promise in Ephesians 2:7 has already materialized in our lives as believers. Upon salvation, we have been blessed with God's grace and kindness. Still, in the coming ages, this very grace and kindness will be the evidence of our salvation when we finally see glory and are face to face with Jesus.

What does this mean? It means that salvation is for the blessing of believers, but even more so, it is for God's glory, both now and in the ages to come. His choice to lavish the immeasurable riches of His grace and kindness upon us is fully realized not on this side of heaven, but on the other, and it will not just be those who are in Christ that will glorify Him for this gift, but the whole of heaven does and will glorify Him for what He has done in rescuing sinners from death and destruction.

Do you grasp the gravity of the riches of His grace? Can you fully comprehend the height, depth, width, and length of this gift? Because the reality of this is that all of heaven and earth will one day glorify God for this act of redemption through His Son Jesus Christ. ALL of heaven and earth. Not one created being will remain standing when every knee bows, and not one mouth will remain silent when every tongue confesses that Jesus Christ is Lord. Not one.

Take a moment and read Revelation 7:9-12. What scene is being described here? What is taking place in the heavenly realms? What is being ascribed to God? Write out these verses and take a few minutes to reflect and meditate on these truths.

First, we can expect future blessing from God if we are in Christ.

Second, the blessing of our salvation is primarily for God's glory and always will be.

Third, we have hope in knowing that one day, ALL will confess that Jesus Christ is Lord, and ALL will bend the knee to the One and Only God of heaven and earth. One day, God will set all things right. One day.

So, we wait. We eagerly anticipate. We expect God. He is who He says He is in His Word, and He will do what He says He will do in His Word. Expect God today.

WEEK FOUR

DAY 3
TIME FOR REFLECTION

1. I believe that Psalm 37 can be summed up in two words: trust and wait. Trust that God's promises are true. Wait on the fulfillment of His promises with eager expectation. Each verse in this Psalm is either speaking of our need to trust in the Lord or to wait on Him or both. Read through Psalm 37 and write next to each verse either the word "trust" or "wait."

2. Do you ever find yourself "expecting God?" When reading His Word? In worship? If not, how can you start living expectantly?

3. The promise of Christ's return is THE promise I await most. To see Him face to face is something that I can only imagine what it will be like. To be rid of this world and its sorrows...I can only imagine how glorious that will be. Read Revelation 21:4 and write it out below. What comforts you most from this verse?

DAY 4
FOR BY GRACE

 "For by grace you have been saved through faith. And this is not your own doing; it is the gift of God, not a result of works, so that no one may boast." EPHESIANS 2:8-9

Considering how much consequence I have found myself in the middle of because of my own poor choices at times, I find it tremendously comforting that at least this one thing is "not my own doing." Salvation is a gift from God. For once, I didn't do it. It can't be earned or deserved, and there's nothing that we do or can do that allows us to obtain any measure of it. For by grace we have been saved. It is only and will only ever be because of God's grace.

As I studied these two verses further, there was an incredible truth that leapt off the page and planted deep roots within my heart. The phrase in verse 8 that says "and this" refers not only to the previous statement of salvation that we have been given and to the grace that has saved us, but it also refers to the faith. Let me unpack this for us. Although we are required to believe in Christ to obtain salvation through Him, even the faith to believe is part of the gift that God gives us. Faith itself is a gift from God and cannot be exercised by our own power apart from God granting it to us. Wow. Do you understand this? Every single one of us that would say, "I have faith in God" must also understand that the faith that enabled us to believe, in order for us to be saved—that very faith was given to us from God. What grace! What mercy that He allowed us to believe! For it is because of God's grace that you were given the faith to believe, and it was that very gift of faith to believe that ushered you into the gift of salvation that Christ extends to all who believe. Further, this salvation was granted because of God's grace. None of this could be had apart from the abundant gift of God's grace. None of it. Just allow that to soak in for a moment. This means that you and I could never come to God on our own merit. He draws us in. We could never choose Him without Him first choosing us. We could never believe in Him without Him first granting us the faith to believe. He is the initiator. He is the Creator. He is the sustainer. He invites us in.

Romans 3:20 speaks further to this and gives us a deeper understanding of God's grace and its role in our faith. What does it say? Can we be saved by our works or our adherence to the Law? Who justifies us? What does Romans 3:28 add to this conversation? What about Galatians 2:16? Look up these verses and record your answers below.

The reason why this conversation is so important is that it is vital to our relationship with Christ. Even among the church, there is a heavy weight of religion that is found, and God's people are oppressed under its burden. God has and always will call us into relationship, not religion. Religion emphasizes all that YOU must do in order to secure good standing with God, and while our works are evidence of genuine, saving faith (James 2:17, 26), they do not save us. Our works are simply expressions of the grace, faith, and salvation that we have received, the overflow of a blessed life. Grace alone secures our fate. For it is by grace. Religion emphasizes your works (plural). Relationship emphasizes God's work (singular).

I don't know where you stand today on this fence. Are you slipping into the dry, desert places of religion, the heavy burden that emphasizes your performance? Or do you find yourself free-falling into the embrace of relationship with Christ? The pastures of God's grace do not exclude the responsibility on our part to pursue obedience and righteous living. Rather, it frees us to know and believe that the obedient life is not the catalyst in securing our salvation, rather the expression of the grateful heart that has been rescued from the grips of sin.

For by grace you have been saved. Not by works. Not by good deeds. Not by sheer determination to stop sinning. Not by volunteering and serving. Not by living a perfect life.

For by grace.

Know that God is inviting you into this freedom today—freedom from religion and the fear that accompanies it; freedom from a heavy load and an impossible yoke. For by grace—faith, salvation, and freedom have come.

WEEK FOUR

DAY 4
TIME FOR REFLECTION

1. There is tremendous freedom that comes when we finally understand and receive God's grace. The heavy burden of religion is lifted when we embrace relationship. Read Matthew 11:28-30. What do we receive when we come to Christ and lay our burdens down?

2. Good works cannot produce salvation, but they are a result of it. Read John 15:8 and write it out below. What is the proof or evidence that we are disciples of Christ?

3. Read Titus 2:11-14. When grace appeared, what did it bring for all people? What fruit did it produce within us who would receive it?

4. Galatians 5:22-23 lists the fruit of the Spirit, behaviors and characteristics that should be increasing in measure in the lives of ALL believers. List them below. Which fruit are you lacking in your life and desire to see more of as you grow in the Lord?

DAY 5
THE EVIDENCE OF FAITH

 "For we are His workmanship, created in Christ Jesus for good works, which God prepared beforehand, that we should walk in them." EPHESIANS 2:10

Have you ever found yourself at a crossroads, two decisions laid out before you, knowing that each decision would ultimately lead you down a different road? You were desperate to make the "right" decision and remain within "God's will" for your life. You were scared to death that if you made the wrong decision, your life, as you know it, would be doomed.

Perhaps I am being too dramatic, but maybe I'm not. I think many believers tend to think in these extremes when it comes to decision-making, and we live fearful that somehow we could wander outside of what God wills for our lives. If we understand sovereignty accurately, we find that there really is no need to fear, because God is in control of the outcome. Not only are we predestined in Him, but He also has predestined good works for us to walk in. Before you took your first breath, He had plans for your life. Before your parents ever thought of the possibility of you, God had good works planned out for you to walk in. I'm not suggesting that you and I are puppets, and that God holds the strings. I'm saying that we can rest in the fact that since He is in control, He is also able to make messages out of our messes. When we screw up and wander, He is able to turn that brokenness into blessing, not only for us, but also for others.

Psalm 139 poetically describes this truth. God's loving hands knit us together in our mothers' wombs. We are fearfully and wonderfully made. (Psalm 139:14) Because He is the master designer and the awesome Creator, we as His workmanship are without flaw. Sin is our natural bent because of the Fall, and it infects us all, but God did not make a mistake when He fashioned and formed us. Not one.

He didn't create us to only be beautiful reflections of His image. There is much more to it than that. He also created us to do good works, works that would boast of His goodness, grace, and love, works that would draw others to Himself. Just as He foreknew us, He also prepared in advance these good works for us to walk in. I love that our God is detail-oriented, because I so am not. He didn't miss a single thing. I always miss things. He never overlooked even the smallest detail. I constantly forget details, even important ones. He was incredibly intentional when He breathed life into our lungs. As He fashioned and formed each one of us in our mothers' wombs, He breathed purpose and meaning into our bones.

This is quite possibly the truth that I find most hope in—that in Christ, I have a purpose. If we are honest with ourselves, every single one of us has wondered at one point in time or another at what our purpose is here on earth. Why? Because we were created on purpose, with purpose, and for purpose. Therefore, we desire to know our purpose. Well, here it is:

Your purpose is to walk in the good works that God has prepared in advance for you.

Every opportunity you're given on this side of heaven to bring Him glory, walk in it. Every person that crosses your path that you can speak life into and truth to, walk in it. Every difficult situation that presents itself, giving you the choice to either trust in the Lord or to run from Him, choose to walk in the good work that was prepared in advance for you. Choose trust. Why is this so incredibly important? When we walk in the good works that God prepared in advance for us to walk in, we bring God glory, and that, my friends, is our highest calling and ultimate purpose: to glorify God. We exist to bring Him glory. That's it. Whatever you do, whether in word or deed, do it all to bring God glory, and as we walk in the good works He prepared for us, the authenticity of our faith is made evident to all. As we walk in the good works He prepared for us, we are transformed, moment by moment and day by day, into the likeness of Jesus Christ. This is the evidence of our faith.

WEEK FOUR

DAY 5
TIME FOR REFLECTION

1. In the event that you might still be thinking that this promise of good works somehow passed over you, read 2 Timothy 3:16-17 and write it out below.

2. Essentially, 2 Timothy 3:16-17 is telling us that God's Word has the power to thoroughly equip us for every good work. How has this proven true in your life? What good works have you been equipped for? What good works are you walking in today?

3. When it comes to this topic of our purpose in Christ, I know that my tendency is to compare my purpose and calling to others', assuming that certain "good works" are better than others because more people see them. Instead, I believe that God calls each and every one of us to a James 1:22 life of purpose, calling, and obedience. Read James 1:22 and write it out below. How is our obedience to this verse fulfilling the "good works" that God prepared in advance for us?

4. We're almost halfway through *Awake O Sleeper*. In what ways have you seen transformation in your own life since the beginning of this study?

week five
WE'VE BEEN BROUGHT NEAR

TEACHING OUTLINE

WEEK 5
WE'VE BEEN BROUGHT NEAR

EPHESIANS 2:11-22

1 Our greatest __gift/*love*__ next to bringing God glory should be bringing the __Lost__ to His feet. (verses 11-13)

2 Choose to be defined by God's __Love__ instead of your __Preferences__. (verses 14-16)
   more about others

3 If we __understood__ grace and __embrace__ it for ourselves, we would never try to __withhold__ it from others. (verse 17-22)

4 When you love __the rules__ more than you love __Jesus__, people become _____ and relationship becomes __religion__.
   Matth 11:28

If you have committed to write out the book of Ephesians, take a few minutes right now to write Ephesians 2:11-22 in the back of your workbook.

DAY 1
THE PRISONER FOR CHRIST

 "For this reason I, Paul, a prisoner for Christ Jesus on behalf of you Gentiles—assuming that you have heard of the stewardship of God's grace that was given to me for you, how the mystery was made known to me by revelation, as I have written briefly." EPHESIANS 3:1-3

There have only been a handful of things in this life that have captured my heart so much so that a significant part of me has become characterized and even arrested by them. From the time I was four, I could be found on some type of sports field. Since my junior high years, it wouldn't be uncommon to find a cup of coffee in my hands. Yes, it's true. From the age of fifteen to the present, few things have seized my passions more than filling my passport with stamps while traveling the world and embracing new cultures, foods, and faces. My mid-twenties began the journey that would mark me for a lifetime—meeting, falling in love with, and saying "I do" to my Jeremy.

Even still, there was a capturing of my heart unlike all the rest that began in my late teenage years and arrests me still to this day. The love of God is far greater than anything I could grasp or taste on this side of heaven. Nothing touches it, and I believe the apostle Paul understood this down to the very fibers of his being. Having spent much of his days after meeting Jesus in peril, under some form of persecution, or imprisoned, he writes with such authority, confidence, and unwavering commitment to the One he suffers for, and there is no amount of difficulty that could change his mind on this: He is a prisoner for Christ. Whether in chains or free, Paul's life mission was to boldly and authoritatively make known the mystery of the Gospel.

Although he wrote these very words to the church in Ephesus while in prison in Rome, notice that his description of himself is not "a prisoner of Rome" or any other government or authority on earth. He defines himself always as "a prisoner for Christ Jesus." Paul wholeheartedly knew that Christ was in control of his every moment. There was a certainty within Paul that caused his ministry to be marked with such confidence in the face of trial because he knew whose hands his life rested in, down to the very details. While he suffered imprisonment because of his ministry to the Gentiles, the final authority over his life came from Jesus Christ.

It is altogether appropriate and fitting for Paul to then address his calling in verse 2 as a "stewardship of God's grace." He doesn't claim the abilities or work given to him as his own doing; rather, he makes known to all who will read this widely circulated letter that whatever grace or gift that rests on his life is the direct result of stewardship. God had entrusted to Paul the authority and leadership over the church that he had, and therefore, Paul understood his responsibility to steward it well.

Do you see the importance of all of this yet? The significance of Paul understanding that he was a prisoner to none other than Jesus Christ allowed him to steward well the gifts and calling that had been given to him. Had he wandered into doubt in regards to who held him captive, we may not have the majority of the New Testament within our reach. Paul's understanding of his identity in Christ determined his activity in life. Don't miss that! The understanding and embracing of who we are in Christ will determine our activity on this side of heaven. When we face difficulty, if we understand the very same truth that Paul did, we are capable of walking in confidence and using every moment of our hardship to bring God glory and to further His church here on earth. There is no telling what our lives could amount to under the authority of Jesus Christ and with the understanding that all we have been given was intended to be stewarded well.

How would our lives change if we lived according to this? If we really grasped whose we are and the value of what has been entrusted to us, this world would be a drastically different place. Try filling in your name in place of Paul's:

_____

A PRISONER FOR CHRIST JESUS ON BEHALF OF...

If your life were marked by such a claim, what on earth could possibly stand in your way?

WEEK FIVE

DAY 1
TIME FOR REFLECTION

1   Read 2 Corinthians 4:8-9 and write out these verses below.

2   In regards to being entrusted with grace and calling in this life, what does 1 Corinthians 12:7 confirm for all believers?

3   _____ (your name), a prisoner for Christ Jesus on behalf of… . In your own life, what or who do you think would finish this sentence? On behalf of whom are you a prisoner for Christ?

DAY 2
THE MYSTERY OF THE GOSPEL

 "When you read this, you can perceive my insight into the mystery of Christ, which was not made known to the sons of men in other generations as it has now been revealed to His holy apostles and prophets by the Spirit. This mystery is that the Gentiles are fellow heirs, members of the same body, and partakers of the promise in Christ Jesus through the gospel."

EPHESIANS 3:4-6

Grace has always amazed me. Not only are we unable to do anything to deserve it, but it is lavished on us abundantly in our undeserving state. While there is an aspect of grace that I can understand, much of its essence will remain a mystery to me because I simply cannot grasp the "why" of it. Why would God grant me His grace? Why would I be chosen to be an heir and partaker of the promise in Christ Jesus? This is the mystery of the Gospel. This is grace.

It is upon this platform of grace that we will build a deeper understanding today. For hundreds of years, the nation of Israel knew that they were God's chosen people. Then came Jesus Christ and His fulfillment of the Law. His life, death, and resurrection secured the promise given to us in Isaiah 49:6, which foretold that salvation would be made available to people of all races. Still, even with this Old Testament promise, the idea of Gentiles being welcomed into God's family was so difficult for many Jews to embrace. It was so seemingly opposed to everything they had ever known.

Paul understood the importance of addressing this mystery that Jew and Gentile were brought together in Christ, especially because his ministry was primarily to the Gentiles. This was a dividing issue within the first church, so Paul not only talked about it, but he explained and clarified this truth. He knew that in order for spiritual truth to be applied properly, it must be accurately explained. You can't just tell people what to do without explaining why because it will rarely produce the intended result. Lists of dos and don'ts are nothing more than a heavy weight of legalism and religion.

How do you think this applies to our lives today? For those of us who grew up in the church, we were given many don'ts. Much of my adolescence was marked by teaching about all of the bad things that I shouldn't do, and a much lesser emphasis was placed on the good that I should be doing. This leaves one entering into adulthood with a warped understanding of who God is—a God who only says no and then waits to strike you with lightning when you mess up. It's nothing more than another brand of religion. If we go back to the truths of Scripture, we find that God gives us good reason for the boundaries that He sets up for us in His Word. And for the good that He does call us to do, He also grants explanation.

The mystery of the Gospel in Ephesians 3 is all about illuminating the grace of God. What was once closed off has now been opened. What once was limited in its reaches is now limitless. To ALL who have received Him and to ALL who have believed in His name, He chooses to call His children (John 1:12). Jew and Gentile alike have become one in God's family. There is no longer any distinction. We all stand shoulder to shoulder as equals in Christ.

This truth puts so much into perspective. If we are in Christ, we are all equal in His sight. And if the Gentile is equally welcomed into the fold along with the Jew, then the principle we can take from this is that there is no one too far for the reaches of God's grace. There is no one who is beyond hope. If there is breath in their lungs, there is hope for their soul. Never stop being full of the blend of grace and truth. Never stop praying for those who do not yet believe. Because we hold fast to the hope that is found within the mystery of the Gospel—though we don't deserve it, grace is freely given.

WEEK FIVE

1. The mystery of the Gospel that Paul is addressing here is that salvation has now been made available to Gentiles. In our day, this may not seem all that shocking, since we have been taught of God's grace for centuries now. This was news, however, to the first church. Read Colossians 1:24-29. In verse 28, what is Paul's intended result of preaching the Good News to all?

2. Withholding grace from others is not a new thing, either. This is a sin that mankind has struggled with for all of time. In what ways are you quick to make judgments on others and refuse to offer grace?

3. Matthew 10:8 paints a clear picture of the heart of God. Jesus tells His disciples here that since they have been freely given grace, forgiveness, healing, and so much more, they should freely give of what has been given to them. Is there someone in your life from whom you are withholding grace? Below, write a prayer of confession, asking God to give you the grace to extend to them. Freely you have received. Now, freely give.

DAY 3
A GENUINE HUMILITY

 "Of this gospel I was made a minister according to the gift of God's grace, which was given me by the working of His power. To me, though I am the very least of all the saints, this grace was given, to preach to the Gentiles the unsearchable riches of Christ, and to bring to light for everyone what is the plan of the mystery hidden for ages in God who created all things, so that through the church the manifold wisdom of God might now be made known to the rulers and authorities in the heavenly places."

EPHESIANS 3:7-10

Whenever I find myself in conversations about the Bible with non-believers, what seems to inevitably come up is this thinking that the Bible is inconsistent with itself, that it somehow contradicts itself. As I've grown in my understanding of God's Word and studied it more for myself, I have found this thinking to be completely inaccurate. Paul, the writer of most of our New Testament, was so consistent in his writings, and the more I study the book of Ephesians, the more amazed I am. The truth that he addresses in Ephesians 3:7-10 is repeated throughout his writings, and he was repeatedly found with genuine humility.

If anyone had an accurate perception of himself, it was Paul. Although he had every earthly reason to boast in his own résumé (2 Corinthians 11:22-29), he constantly reminded himself and his readers that he was "the very least of all the saints." At first glance, I see how it would be easy to assume this was a false humility in Paul. Who calls themselves the least and the worst so frequently, especially someone in church leadership? As I dug a bit deeper, though, all I could find is this:

An accurate understanding of who God is produces genuine humility within us.

Formerly, Paul was a persecutor of the church and all who followed after Christ. Now, he is being persecuted for his faith in Jesus. After having been dramatically converted on the road to Damascus, Paul became fearless in his ministry to the lost. Why? Because he fully understood the depth of grace that rescued him from a life of waywardness, he remained constantly aware of who God is and who he (Paul) was not. Paul knew he was nothing without the power of Christ at work within him, which is the reason he so often stated his ranking in the Kingdom—not to discredit himself, but much rather to showcase the good God who was at work within him.

This begs the question for us today, "How do we respond to praise?" Paul certainly received praise throughout his ministry to the church, but it's what he did with that praise that made all the difference in the world. Instead of absorbing the praises of man, he deflected them to the only One who truly deserved them: Jesus Christ. This is not a false humility; it's genuine. When we desire God to be honored and glorified more than seeking our own recognition, we finally find ourselves in a right place, the best place—genuine humility. Are you often found here? Bowed low, understanding who God is and who you're not, and desiring nothing more than bringing Him praise? Because an accurate understanding of who God is produces genuine humility in us.

WEEK FIVE

DAY 3
TIME FOR REFLECTION

1. Read Philippians 2:1-11. This passage is Jesus Christ's example of humility for us to follow. Write out Philippians 2:3 below.

2. In what ways will you purpose to put others' needs before your own today? This week?

3. An accurate understanding of who God is produces genuine humility in us. Why is this statement true?

4. Isaiah 6 records a vision of the Lord that Isaiah was given. His response of being found in the presence of the Lord was one of utter humility. Read Isaiah 6:1-7 and write out Isaiah's response from verse 5 below.

DAY 4
THE TYPE OF CONFIDENCE WE NEED

 "This was according to the eternal purpose that he has realized in Christ Jesus our Lord, in whom we have boldness and access with confidence through our faith in Him." EPHESIANS 3:11-12

I recently attended an absolutely amazing wedding—the kind of wedding that will not soon, if ever, be forgotten. There was incredible beauty in each and every detail, great times were had by all, and countless pictures were taken. Although I took nearly one hundred pictures throughout the day, there were still others who captured moments that I missed. As we all began sharing our pictures on various forms of social media, something struck me. Most of these pictures had groups of people in them. However, each time I came across a photo that I was in, instead of taking in the entire shot, my eyes focused in immediately on myself. Before even glancing at the other faces that surrounded me, I was set on finding each and every flaw or slight imperfection in myself. I think if I polled a crowd, most if not all would also say that they tend to look first at themselves before scanning the entire picture.

While this is a very simple and perhaps generalized example, there is a truth to be found here. We live in a world that is obsessed with self and is constantly feeding us the doctrine of the importance of self-confidence. As I read through Paul's message to the church in Ephesus again today, the single word that leaps off of the page at me more than the rest is "confidence." Through Christ, we have been given direct access to God. If we are in Christ, we are no longer separated from God because His Spirit lives within us. There is no human being that needs to intercede for us any longer because Christ is our intercessor. This should give us confidence, not in ourselves, but rather in Christ.

There are great differences between what the world would deem as wisdom and what God's Word defines as wisdom. The world tells us that we must love ourselves. Jesus told us to first love Him and to then love others. The world tells us that we deserve all or most of the things that we want. Jesus tells us that while we don't deserve grace, it has been freely given to us. The world tells us that we need to be confident in ourselves in order to succeed in life. Jesus tells us to be confident in Him, and our reward will be in the next life. If we, as followers of Christ, could embrace a new mentality that says, "More of you, Jesus, and less of me," we would see a decrease in self-confidence and an increase in Christ-confidence.

As I write these very words, my heart is heavy for someone I love very much who is trapped in a place of self-condemnation. While this person believes in God, there is also this warped belief that is present that causes them to feel that before they can come to God, they must clean up their act first. If they aren't self-confident, then they feel they can't come at all. Because of the cross of Jesus Christ, we have been given free access to God at any time, and we can come to Him with confidence—not a self-confidence in all that we have done or can do for God, but rather a Christ-confidence in all that Jesus has already done for us.

I imagine that many of you, if not all, come to the pages of Scripture with me today battling some form of insecurity or lack of confidence. Hear this truth today that will usher freedom into your soul. The confidence that you lack and are desperately looking for is found in one place.

In Christ alone.

In Christ alone, we have been given access to God.

In Christ alone, we have hope.

In Christ alone, we have an assurance of salvation.

Therefore, we can possess confidence in all things. He is in us. He is for us. He is with us. Remember this and walk in the Christ-confidence that you've been given.

WEEK FIVE

DAY 4
TIME FOR REFLECTION

1. Read Jeremiah 17:7 in the New International Version and write it out below.

2. Paul spoke of humility in the flesh and confidence in Christ on more than one occasion. Read Philippians 3:1-11. We read a portion of "Paul's résumé" here, but we hear him dismiss it as worthless compared to "the surpassing worth of knowing Christ Jesus." In what areas are you tempted to put confidence in the flesh or in your own abilities and not in Christ alone?

3. I love the book of Hebrews. There is so much rich truth packed into its pages, and I've spent countless hours poring over its words. Hebrews 10:19-23 reminds us of the confidence that is ours in Christ. Take a moment to read through these verses for yourself. Which verse stands out to you most and why?

4. We need not fear when approaching the throne of grace because it is a place where we have been invited to come. In Christ, we have been washed clean from the stains of our pasts. What is the command we are given in Hebrews 10:22?

5. Spend some time now "drawing near to God." Below, journal a prayer of response to the Lord, thanking Him for what He's taught you today.

DAY 5
DON'T GIVE UP

 "So I ask you not to lose heart over what I am suffering for you, which is your glory." EPHESIANS 3:13

Although it's now been a few years, sometimes it feels like yesterday when I was training for my first half marathon. During the first few weeks of my training, running seemed to be the most difficult thing in my life. I never wanted to run. I groaned every day when I got out of bed in the morning to go hit the pavement. It was such a hard discipline for me. A few weeks into the training, however, I began to notice a change not only in my attitude toward running but also in how I felt physically. I was beginning to look forward to running. This discipline had somehow transformed into desire. If I missed even one day for any reason, my entire schedule seemed off. When I had finally allowed the discipline of training to produce the desired results within me, I was able to be grateful for the difficult and painful times.

Isn't this so similar to our lives? In hindsight, we are able to see how the hard times were able to bring about good, whether it was in us or in others, and we can somehow be thankful for it. Scripture is consistent with this principle, as well. Not only are we promised hardship in this life, but we are also instructed to consider it joy when we face these trials. (James 1:2) Therefore, it's not a matter of "if" difficulty will enter into our lives but rather "when" it will, and when it does, we are told that it is not impossible for us to still be found with joy. When our circumstances threaten to steal our hope and joy, will we be found among those who persevere or among those who give up?

Paul's audience knew well of his conditions, and although Paul wanted them to be aware of what he was going through for the sake of the Gospel, the last thing he wanted was for them to lose heart over his sufferings. Were they to grow weary and faint over what Paul was going through, the very real temptation for them then would be to give up. Being a follower of Jesus Christ was never intended to be easy, but it was especially difficult for those who were a part of the first church in the New Testament. Persecution was a very real and constant threat to them, and this is why Paul spent much, if not all, of his time in prison writing letters of hope, encouragement, and truth to the churches. Much of Paul's message was one of challenge and exhortation to persevere through whatever would befall the believer.

This is precisely why I run to his writings that fill the New Testament because this message is just as much needed today as it was two thousand years ago. Although most of Western Christianity is not exposed to religious persecution, our brothers and sisters in Christ around the globe often live under the constant threat of death because of their faith. While we, for the most part, are not undergoing such intense persecution for our faith, I have found that many choose to "give up" for even lesser reasons. Life gets hard, and rather than clinging to our hope and security who is the person of Jesus Christ, the tendency seems to be either pointing the finger of blame at God or running from Him. How can we so easily walk away from the very commitment that introduced hope into our existence and changed our lives forever?

My last intention would be to minimize the hardship that any single one of you is facing. There are pains and trials that many of you have tasted in this life that I cannot begin to fathom. Still, there is a God who is greater and significantly more powerful than the deepest pain we could ever experience on this earth. I have tasted pain. I have dwelt in some very deep valleys, but I have also rested in the arms of grace. These very words of hope that I write to you today come from the precious promises that we are given in His Word. Although we will endure suffering to some degree here on this earth, we have the hope of glory.

Friend, don't give up. Don't stop running your race now. The finish line is in sight. The hope of glory is but a breath away. The battle will be won, and we will be found on the victorious side of the fight if we but persevere. Our God is true to His Word. One day, we will sing in unison, "Oh death, where is your sting?" The war on death has been waged, and our God has overcome. One day, all things will be made right. One day, there will be no more tears and no more sorrow. One day, our faith will be made sight.

And until that day, press on. Don't give up. Cling to the pierced side of your Savior.

WEEK FIVE

DAY 5
TIME FOR REFLECTION

1. What threatens you to lose heart today in your fight to remain faithful?

2. Read 2 Corinthians 4:17 and write it out below. What words are used in this verse to describe our affliction or troubles here on earth? How does this put our sufferings into perspective?

3. We are given many promises throughout Scripture that give us hope to cling to when life hurts. What promise are we given in Romans 8:28?

week six
A POWERFUL PRAYER

TEACHING OUTLINE

WEEK 6
A POWERFUL PRAYER

EPHESIANS 3:14-21

1 _____ to and _____ for God in prayer should _____ the life of the believer. (verses 14-15)

2 We need _____ _____ to comprehend the greatness of God's love for us. (verses 16-19)

3 Because God is able to do far more than we could imagine, our _____ should be a _____ of this. (verses 20-21)

If you have committed to write out the book of Ephesians, take a few minutes right now to write Ephesians 3:14-21 in the back of your workbook.

DAY 1
TO WALK WORTHY

 "I therefore, a prisoner for the Lord, urge you to walk in a manner worthy of the calling to which you have been called, with all humility and gentleness, with patience, bearing with one another in love, eager to maintain the unity of the Spirit in the bond of peace."

EPHESIANS 4:1-3

As I type these words today, I'm reminded of the inevitability of transitions in life. When one chapter ends, another begins. My family and I just said a very tearful goodbye to my dear sister and her new husband on a train station platform in Nuremberg, Germany, and we are now in the middle of our trek to Berlin. Tomorrow, we will fly over the ocean back home, and while this journey has been nothing short of wonderful, a new chapter will begin in a few days that I'm eager to start.

It's not all that surprising to me then, that our journey through Ephesians also begins a new chapter, tone, and direction today as we open up chapter four. "Therefore" in verse 1 signifies the transition from the teaching of doctrine and position to the teaching of practice and behavior. After three chapters of addressing who Christ is, who we are in Christ, and what we should believe because of it, we enter into Paul's instruction on how to live our lives accordingly. Buckle up, friends. This is going to be a challenging and exciting ride. Life change is about to happen if we choose to submit ourselves to the teaching of God's Word. Three more chapters of Ephesians lie ahead of us. Are you with me?

This isn't the first time in Ephesians that Paul mentions his imprisonment, and he does so here again to remind his readers that there is a cost that comes with following Christ. Knowing that, he wants them to still choose a life of obedience, one that is worthy of the calling. The command to "walk worthy" is where I would like us to park for our time together today. Throughout the New Testament, the word "walk" is often used to refer to daily conduct or behavior, and this one word sets the stage for the remainder of the book. This is Paul's way of introducing practical application. He doesn't want them to only possess head knowledge. He desires heart change. The word "worthy" encompasses the idea of living a life consistent with your position in Christ, meaning that your walk should match your talk.

The command given is clear: "Walk worthy." Still, Paul's pastoral heart shines through as he follows up this command with a detailed description of what it would look like for them to obey this command. It starts with humility, a word not even found in the Greek vocabulary of Paul's day. Christ's life introduced this virtue. To be like Christ is to be humble; therefore, it is quite possibly the most foundational of the Christian virtues. After laying the foundation of humility, Paul builds upon that with gentleness. If we walk in humility, gentleness (or meekness) is a natural byproduct—gentleness in our words, actions, relationships, etc. Then comes the virtue of patience, which is also a result of humility and gentleness. Patience and gentleness are fruits of the Spirit, thus a result of walking closely with the Lord. Finally, if we walk in these virtues, our final destination and end result will always be love. This is what it looks like to "walk worthy" of our calling.

Be humble.

Be gentle.

Be patient.

Be love.

If the body of Christ were marked by these virtues, this world would be a drastically different place. If the church were marked by these virtues, our seats would be full and our buildings would be bursting at their seams. If you and I were marked by these virtues, there is no telling the impact we could have for God's Kingdom here on this earth.

Christian, the call today is to walk worthy. Represent Jesus well. Be the city on a hill for all to see.

WEEK SIX

DAY 1
TIME FOR REFLECTION

1. In regards to the command we are given in Ephesians 4:1 to "walk worthy," in what ways do you think that Christ is most misrepresented in our world today?

2. Read Colossians 2:6-7 and write out these verses below.

3. In Colossians 3:12-14, we can see the same progression of virtuous living in this passage: humility, gentleness, patience, and love. Verse 12 begins with the command to "put on" or to "clothe yourselves." What practical application needs to take place in your life today in order for you to be clothed with these godly virtues?

4. An essential part of a worthy walk is the pursuit of peace and unity with members of the body of Christ. This is an impossible reality without love. Love binds us together in unity and in peace. 1 Corinthians 13:4-8a gives us the perfect definition of love. Read these verses and write them out below. Which part of the description of love stands out to you most and why?

DAY 2
THE MODEL FOR UNITY

 "There is one body and one Spirit—just as you were called to the one hope that belongs to your call—one Lord, one faith, one baptism, one God and Father of all, who is over all and through all and in all."

EPHESIANS 4:4-6

In my thirty-two years, I have been a part of or attended countless denominations within the Christian church, each distinct in its own way. Some differ in their expressions of worship, some in their style of teaching, and some in their theology and interpretation of Scripture. A great divide exists within the body of Christ today, for reasons as large as who Jesus Christ is defined to be and for reasons as small as the preference of pews over chairs in the worship center. This vastly unbelieving world takes one look at Christianity and by and large shakes its head in disbelief.

How is it that we have strayed so far from unity? How is it that the church has created more divides than built bridges? When we find ourselves scratching our own heads in wonder and disbelief over the current state of the church, our default and our first stop must be God's Word. It is the lamp unto our feet and the light to our paths, and it speaks to even this.

Again, the backdrop for Paul's letter to the Ephesians is the reality of false teachers in their midst. Therefore, he spent the first half of the letter reminding them of solid, theological truths that would propel them into obedient living. The point he emphasized for them two thousand years ago and for us today is this: Unity. It is absolutely essential for us to believe that even though we live in a very conflicted world when it comes to faith, unity within the body of Christ is not only possible, but it is our mandate.

The essential problem that is the common denominator in all of our sin is pride. Pride creeps into the hearts of even the most devout believers and lies to us repeatedly, causing us to believe that we have the authority to redefine what unity is and how it is expressed. In so doing, we have stepped out from under the authority of God's Word on the matter because Scripture has already shown us how to live unified within the church. Here in Ephesians 4:4-6, Paul outlines this for us by using the Trinity as our model for unity: The Holy Spirit in verse four, the Son in verse five, and God the Father in verse six. Although each person of the Trinity is unique in their role, they stand completely unified in every area: one body, one hope, one Lord, one faith, one baptism, one God. Likewise, we should follow suit.

The church at large has different functions as well. Without straying from the message of the Gospel of Jesus Christ in any way, each church should seek to meet the needs of their demographic and reach their community. There will always be non-negotiables when it comes to faith in Jesus Christ (for example: one way, one truth, one life), but I believe we err when we throw stones at those whose expression of their beliefs differs from our own. If we, as the body of Christ, stopped looking at the Bible-believing church down the street as our competition but rather as our teammate, perhaps unity would begin to define us more. If we began to pray for an outpouring of the Holy Spirit, the same Spirit that dwells in every believer upon conversion, to fall on every church in our community, state, country, and world, perhaps unity would begin to define us more. If we began to preach with our lives that there is one God and only one way to Him instead of bowing down to tolerance and the need to be politically correct, perhaps unity would begin to define us more. And if we, as the body of Christ, stopped looking to the things of this world to provide us with hope and security, and rather remembered that we have been given One Hope in Christ which is all that we need, perhaps unity would begin to define us more.

To the believers who find themselves conflicted over the constant divides within the body of Christ, remember this: Our final authority on all matters in this life should always come from God's Word and not man's. Strive for unity. Look to the Father, the Son, and the Spirit as your model for unity. And remember this: If we are in Christ, we are one in Him.

WEEK SIX

DAY 2
TIME FOR REFLECTION

1. In 1 Corinthians 12, Paul writes about the spiritual gifts that are given to believers. While these gifts differ from one another, his emphasis is that although we are many differing parts, we form one body. Read 1 Corinthians 12:11 and write it out below.

2. We live in a world that emphatically claims that there are many ways one can take to get to God. Even the definition of God differs from one religion to another. Read Acts 4:12. Who is this verse talking about? How is this verse consistent with the teaching in Ephesians 4:4-6?

3. God possesses many attributes, and one of them is jealousy. Our God is a jealous God, meaning that He will not share His glory with another. Even Old Testament teaching was consistent with this truth. What does Isaiah 43:10-11 tell us about the oneness of God?

4. With the gifts that God has given you, how can you be a tangible expression of unity and peace within your local church?

DAY 3
THE GOSPEL IN ONE WORD

"But grace was given to each one of us according to the measure of Christ's gift. Therefore it says, 'When He ascended on high He led a host of captives, and He gave gifts to men.' (In saying, 'He ascended,' what does it mean but that He had also descended into the lower parts of the earth? He who descended is the one who also ascended far above all the heavens, that He might fill all things.)" EPHESIANS 4:7-10

Grace. The entirety of the Gospel of Jesus Christ woven together in just one word. Unmerited favor. Getting what we don't deserve. *Grace.*

We looked at the call to unity yesterday, and this can only be accomplished by God's grace made manifest in and through us. As much as we are unified in Christ, we are also unique as individual believers in Christ, and the uniqueness of our callings is nothing short of the outpouring of God's grace on our lives as well.

"But grace was given to each one..."

One of the many things that I love about grace is that it cannot be earned. Notice in verse seven that it is given according to the sovereign will and design of God. He decides what is given to whom. Grace depends on Him and what He has already done, not on us nor what we can do. One thing that we can be confident of, though, is that every single believer is a recipient of this grace, and this gift is free. To all who have placed their faith in Jesus Christ, each has been given a unique spiritual gift that is to be used for God's glory and the betterment of His church. We will look more specifically at some of these gifts tomorrow, but for today, rest assured that in Christ, you have been gifted with this grace.

"When He ascended on high..."

The perfect life of Jesus Christ here on this earth made Him the only perfect sacrifice that would atone for the sins of the world. Having gone through the brutality of the cross and having overcome the power of death in the grave, the resurrection of Jesus Christ sealed for all believers for all time the gift of God's grace. Jesus Christ accomplished what He descended into earth to fulfill. The veil was torn in two. The great divide between God and man was bridged. Jesus Christ made a way. Jesus Christ is the way. His position of rule and authority now is seated in the heavens, interceding on our behalf to the Father. He reigns. He is glorified. He is alive. His reign is marked by the grace He pours into our lives. *Grace.*

"...that He might fill all things."

Every aspect of the life of Christ was a fulfillment of Old Testament prophecy. His ascension restored Him to His rightful place, where at the name of Jesus, every knee will bow and every tongue confess that He is Lord (Philippians 2:10). From that moment in time until His long-awaited return, He is filling all things. He rules over the church and gives gifts to His children. Not a single moment passes by on this earth when He is not at work in our midst. Because of His grace, we have been invited to come alongside Him in His redemptive work and plan. Because of His grace, we have been spiritually gifted to accomplish this work. Because of His grace, the lost who surround us can know the hope we possess. The Gospel in one word: *Grace.*

WEEK SIX

DAY 3
TIME FOR REFLECTION

1. The term "Gospel" used in Scripture literally means "good news." The life, death, burial, and resurrection of Jesus Christ is the Gospel. Why is this good news for you?

2. Paul writes again in 1 Corinthians 15 of his unworthiness to be a recipient of God's grace. Even so, God poured grace on Paul's life. He sums this up in 1 Corinthians 15:10. Read this verse and write it out below.

3. Other than the gift of salvation, what gifts has God given you that are expressions of His grace toward you? How are you using these gifts to further His Kingdom here on this earth?

DAY 4
HE GAVE GIFTS

> *"And He gave the apostles, the prophets, the evangelists, the pastors and teachers, to equip the saints for the work of ministry, for building up the body of Christ, until we all attain to the unity of the faith and of the knowledge of the Son of God, to mature manhood, to the measure of the stature of the fullness of Christ, so that we may no longer be children, tossed to and fro by the waves and carried about by every wind of doctrine, by human cunning, by craftiness in deceitful schemes."* EPHESIANS 4:11-14

With knowledge comes responsibility. It was just the other day that I was in a conversation with someone about this very thing. Knowledge, in and of itself, is a gift, and one that many in this world unfortunately go without. It is a gift, but it is also a responsibility. To know and to do nothing with that knowledge is to waste the gift of it. Spiritual gifts are just that—they are gifts freely given to each and every follower of Jesus Christ. These gifts, however, were not given to collect dust. These gifts come with responsibility. We are to use the gifts given to us for God's glory and for His church.

Aside from Ephesians 4, there are three other passages in the New Testament that contain lists of spiritual gifts: Romans 12:6-8, 1 Corinthians 12:4-11, and 1 Peter 4:10-11. While none of these lists is exhaustive in themselves, they complement one another and reveal to us God's design regarding the gifts of the Spirit. Take a moment and read each of these passages.

Today, we're going to look at the four spiritual gifts that we're given in Ephesians 4, starting with the spiritual gift of apostleship. The term "apostle" in Scripture means "sent one" and was particularly reserved for the twelve disciples plus Paul, all of whom had seen the risen Christ in the flesh, or in Paul's case during his conversion on the road to Damascus. Another qualifying factor for apostleship was that they were directly chosen by Christ Himself. They didn't seek this title for themselves; it was given to them. Their primary responsibilities were to lay the foundation of the early church, to receive, declare, and write God's Word, and to perform signs and wonders that would confirm the truth of the Word.

The second gift listed in our Ephesians passage is the gift of prophecy. While this gift in the Old Testament manifested itself most in the foretelling of future events, its expression in the New Testament was more focused on determining what God's will was in certain situations, similar to discernment. Prophecy within the early church of the New Testament existed primarily for work within local congregations. Often times, the office of prophet was used to expound upon or to provide practical application for revelation already given.

The third gift we'll look at today from Ephesians 4 is the gift of evangelism. An evangelist is one who proclaims the good news of Jesus Christ and His salvation to unbelievers. While apostles were responsible for receiving the Word and writing it down, evangelists were responsible for speaking it to any and all who did not yet believe. This is a gift that comes with boldness to proclaim the mystery of the Gospel.

Finally, there are pastors and teachers, two different words here that are used to describe a singular term—an office of leadership within the church. This gift refers to the teaching shepherd, one who oversees the flock.

Don't miss this. These gifts are given for the building up and equipping of the saints. The early believers were at constant risk of being persuaded by false teaching and false prophecy, which isn't all that different from the state of the church today. Those given these gifts were to use them to help prevent this from happening. It comes down to knowing God's Word and doing God's Word. When the body of Christ uses the gifts we have been given, the church is a healthy place to be. When we sit on our gifts, afraid to use them or simply not sure what our gifts are, our light in this dark world is dimmed. God gave us gifts. Use them for His glory. Use them for His people.

WEEK SIX

DAY 4
TIME FOR REFLECTION

1. From the four passages of Scripture we looked at today (Ephesians 4:11-14, Romans 12:6-8, 1 Corinthians 12:4-11, and 1 Peter 4:10-11), make a list below of the spiritual gifts.

2. In light of the above list of spiritual gifts, in what areas are you most passionate about serving the Lord?

3. Over the past several years, the words of Acts 20:24 have become my anthem. I want these words to be true of my life. Whatever the course God has you on or the ministry he has entrusted to you, I pray that you also desire to finish well. Read this verse and write it out below.

DAY 5
WHEN WE SPEAK THE TRUTH IN LOVE

 "Rather, speaking the truth in love, we are to grow up in every way into Him who is the head, into Christ, from whom the whole body, joined and held together by every joint with which it is equipped, when each part is working properly, makes the body grow so that it builds itself up in love." EPHESIANS 4:15-16

Being someone of many, many words, both spoken and written, any time the Bible references our speech, my ears perk up. When I read verses such as Proverbs 10:19 which says, "When words are many, transgression is not lacking, but whoever restrains his lips is prudent," I cannot help but be convicted about my words. Do I think before I speak? Are my words necessary? Do my words bless those who hear them? Living in our world of the internet, blogging, and all forms of social media, we certainly aren't lacking in the words we put out there nor in the words we ingest. While there is little we can do to curb others' words, there is much we can do to control our own. Are your words spoken in love? Written in love? Shared in love?

By this point in our study of Ephesians, we shouldn't be surprised that Paul cares much about sound doctrine. He spent the first half of his letter addressing it to ensure that the Ephesians would avoid Biblical poverty and rather stand on a firm foundation in their faith in Jesus Christ. He also desired that they, too, would rise up and continue spreading the true message of the Gospel, so that all of the world would know the hope which they possessed. There were an abundance of false teachers and false doctrines in circulation, so his emphasis on truth should not be overlooked. Still, his message was to not only speak truth, but rather to speak truth in love. Any one of them, including Paul, at any time, could have stood on the street corners spewing condemnation and hate, but Paul addressed the importance of speaking the truth in love.

Every time Jesus opened His mouth, His words flowed from a place of love. Because Christ is love, His words were and always will be loving. We, on the other hand, are soiled by our sinful nature, and while our words have the power to heal and bring life, they also have the power to curse and bring death. Before we open our mouths, we must always ask ourselves whether or not our driving force is love. What Paul is emphasizing here in verse fifteen is that when the truth is spoken in love, our efforts in sharing the Gospel are most effective. When the truth is spoken from a place of pride or self-righteousness, immeasurable damage is done. Ultimately, this is a matter of spiritual maturity.

A spiritually mature believer is marked by complete submission and obedience to God's Word and His will, and is subject to Him in all areas of life, including speech. Therefore, speaking the truth without spiritual maturity can result in a harsh delivery and can wound the recipient. If we operate our lives under the headship and authority of Jesus Christ, we will find that our spiritual maturity rests not upon our own shoulders and on what we do, but rather on the power of God at work in us, equipping us for every good work, including speaking the truth in love.

Much hinges on this point of obedience. The world needs the truth. There is no doubt about that. The world also needs love. In God's economy, the two cannot be separated. Truth without love is brutal. Love without truth is deceitful. They must go hand in hand, and when they do, the church grows, and the individual believers mature. When we speak the truth in love, we become vessels of God's love, the hope of glory. When we speak the truth in love, a harsh and unloving world finally sees the face of Jesus.

WEEK SIX

1. What characterizes humble, loving speech?

2. Read James 3:9-10 and write out these verses below.

3. What does 2 Timothy 2:24-26 add to our conversation today about speaking the truth in love? What are some of the results of our kind, patient, and gentle speech?

4. In what way has God convicted you today, specifically regarding your speech?

week seven
THE CALL TO NEW LIFE

TEACHING OUTLINE

WEEK 7
THE CALL TO NEW LIFE

EPHESIANS 4:17-24

1 The marks of ungodly living are __Futility__, __Ignorance__, __Calleness__, and __Impurity__. (verses 17-19)

   use/pursue senselessness *lack of knowledge* *hardened*
   control

   work business JAZZ

2 With __Knowledge__ comes __responsibility__. (verses 20-22)

3 When __Head__ knowledge transfers to __♡__ knowledge it culminates in changed __behaviour__. (verses 23-24)

   Not just hearing the word but doers

> If you have committed to write out the book of Ephesians, take a few minutes right now to write Ephesians 4:17-24 in the back of your workbook.

DAY 1
TWO TRUTHS & A LIE

 "Therefore, having put away falsehood, let each one of you speak the truth with his neighbor, for we are members one of another."

EPHESIANS 4:25

Have you ever heard of the game "Two truths and a lie?" Each player has the opportunity to share two true statements or stories about themselves and one lie. The rest of the players then determine which statement was false. I've always viewed this game as a fun way to get to know people and the interesting details about their lives. Depending on the group you're playing with, you can hear some pretty crazy and very hilarious stories! Since I've never been a very good liar, I've had to learn how to embellish the truth when I play this game, taking a true story and adding false details to it. While "Two truths and a lie" is just a game, the unfortunate reality is that many of us have taken this approach in life.

As Paul continues to describe what the new life in Christ looks like, I'm not surprised that he included this one verse about truth telling. Considering that "Thou shall not lie" was also included in the Ten Commandments, I think it's safe to say that this is a pretty big deal to God. The exaggeration of details or half-truths are just as dishonest as telling a blatant lie. In God's economy, where the standard of living is holiness, I think we can dispense with the notion that there is such a thing as a "white lie." A lie is a lie is a lie. It's that simple, and when we distort the truth in any way, we are guilty of this.

Ephesians 4:25 instructs us to "put away falsehood." Cheating, making promises we can't keep, betraying a confidence, offering false excuses, exaggerating the truth, and withholding information are all forms of lying, and these behaviors are not at all fitting for a follower of Jesus Christ. These patterns are the things that marked and characterized our lives before Christ, but they have no place in the life of the believer. Not only is Paul saying that we should not lie, but also that we should take no part in falsehood of any kind. This would include engaging in dishonest conversations, gossip, cutting corners at work, or affording anyone else the opportunity to do so. Some, if not most of these things have become the norm, and to act any differently would almost cause us to stick out like a sore thumb.

Which is exactly the point.

Jesus Christ said, "I am the Way, the Truth, and the Life." Nearly every time He opened His mouth, He would begin by saying, "Truly, truly I say unto you..." Whenever He spoke, He spoke truth. God is a God of truth, and His work in this world is based entirely upon truth. Therefore, if we are not truthful in all things, how can we be fit instruments for the Lord's use? We were never intended to "fit in" with this world. Because we are new creations in Christ, we stand as lights in this world, illuminating the darkness, speaking truth in a world of lies, and standing out, not blending in. This is why Paul emphasizes this here.

Stop lying. Start speaking truth.

We greatly misrepresent Christ when we bear His name and false witness at the same time. While the temptation to lie is great, the power we've been given to overcome temptation is greater. When we choose to operate in falsehood and deceitfulness, we unite ourselves with the father of lies himself, Satan. Lying is his native tongue. Whenever he opens his mouth, lies pour out. We've been called to a higher standard. We've been given a greater purpose. Speak truth, the whole truth, and nothing but the truth. This is the new life you've been called to in Christ. Walk in it.

WEEK SEVEN

DAY 1
TIME FOR REFLECTION

1. Dishonesty is not a back-burner issue with God. This matters greatly to Him. Read Proverbs 6:16-19 and list below the seven things that God hates. How many of these things have to do with lying?

2. Paul is quoting Zechariah 8:16 here in Ephesians 4:25 when he tells us to speak truth. Write out both verses below and underline the phrase "speak the truth" in each verse.

3. In what ways are you guilty of falsehood? How has God convicted your heart on this matter today? Write a prayer of repentance below and commit your tongue to the Lord to be used as an instrument of truth.

DAY 2
WHEN YOU'RE ANGRY

 "Be angry and do not sin; do not let the sun go down on your anger, and give no opportunity to the devil."

EPHESIANS 4:26-27

When was the last time you were angry? When were you last really frustrated, irritated, or annoyed? Last month? Last week? Today? Was it because someone offended you? Was it because someone spoke poorly of you or misrepresented you to others? Did someone betray you, rob you, or turn their back on you? Or was it because someone offended God? Was your anger induced because someone spoke poorly of your Savior or misrepresented Him to others? Was it because someone betrayed the God you love, robbed Him of His glory, and turned their back on Him? When was the last time you were angry, and what was the cause?

We are given many commands throughout Scripture: commands to abstain from evil and commands to do good. Seeing as God does not offer us many suggestions in His Word, we would do well to listen up whenever He instructs us on how we are to live our lives. Ephesians 4:26-27 is no different in that we are given instructions here on how to act when we are angry. However, it actually goes a step further than that. The first two words in verse 26 are a command.

"Be angry."

Ok, hold the phone! You mean to tell me that God is telling us to be angry? Yes, He is. Now, before you run off and starting screaming at your spouse or cussing out the person who cuts you off on the road, take a moment to finish reading. According to Deuteronomy 32:4, all of God's ways and works are perfect, just, and upright. God would never instruct us to say or do anything that isn't good. Therefore, what does Ephesians 4:26 mean, and how are we to appropriately apply this to our lives?

Anger can either be good or bad, righteous or sinful, depending on the driving motivation behind it. A righteous indignation (anger at or against evil, injustice, immorality, and ungodliness) is permissible, but it is not without boundaries. Jesus, Himself, expressed this kind of anger in Matthew 21:12-13 when He overturned the tables in the temple. His anger stemmed from a love for God and a love for His people. The money-changers in the temple were charging astronomical amounts of money for the animals they were selling for sacrifices, thus preventing the poor from worship in God's house. This infuriated Christ that some would prevent others from worshiping the Father. This is a righteous anger.

Unfortunately, our anger often stems from selfishness and pride, and this kind of anger is sinful in God's eyes and without excuse. As much as we would like to be able to justify our sinful emotions based on what others have done to or against us, our excuses will fall flat before a Holy God. The command we are given in Ephesians 4:26-27 is to have a righteous anger—to be angry over what angers the heart of God: sin. Still, even with this instruction, God also included a very specific boundary.

"Do not let the sun go down on your anger."

Being that we are painfully human, the natural state of our hearts is bent on sin. This is precisely why God put a time limit on even a righteous anger. Given enough time, even a godly anger can turn to bitterness and hostility. The reality is that it's incredibly difficult for us to be angry and not sin. Anger is a strong emotion that isn't controlled easily, certainly not without the power of Christ in us. Anger is also an emotion that affects us all, so we need to know what to do when we are angry. The next time you're angry, ask yourself these questions:

1. *Am I angry because I was offended or because God was offended?*
2. *Am I bitter toward the person or angry at their sin?*
3. *Am I entertaining thoughts of repaying evil for the evil that was done against me?*

If we can be honest with ourselves in answering these questions, we would more than likely find that much of our anger should be displaced with repentance. It's not a matter of "if" you'll ever be angry; it's a matter of "when." When you are angry, what will you do with your anger? Every time we operate in sinful anger, we give our enemy opportunity to influence and deceive us. The word "opportunity" in Ephesians 4:27 literally means "a place." Friends, don't give the devil a place to sit at your table. Don't offer him a place to reside in your heart. Don't allow him to have a place in your mind. Be angry, but do not sin in your anger.

WEEK SEVEN

DAY 2
TIME FOR REFLECTION

1 Ephesians 4 is not the only place in Scripture that addresses this issue of anger. Read Psalm 4:4 and write it out below.

2 God knows that anger is a difficult emotion for us to manage well. This is why He gives us Ephesians 4:26-27. When we prolong our anger, we are increasingly susceptible to sin. Read Romans 12:17-21. What further instruction are we given in this passage?

3 When was the last time you were angry? Was it a righteous indignation or a sinful anger?

4 In the space provided below, write a prayer of confession, asking God to forgive you of any ungodly anger that is present in your life. Ask God to give you a heart like His.

DAY 3
HONEST, HARD WORK

 "Let the thief no longer steal, but rather let him labor, doing honest work with his own hands, so that he may have something to share with anyone in need." EPHESIANS 4:28

Have you ever wondered whether or not the people who you work with know that you're a Christian? Better yet, has anyone ever been surprised when they found out that you were? Does your "walk" accurately represent your "talk?" It's a fair question, and it's one that we all must ask ourselves, because one day, God will determine the answer for us. Does every part of your life represent the God you say you follow?

Paul continues in his detailed instruction to the Ephesians in verse 28 on how to live the Christian life well. One of the things I love about Paul is his thoroughness on all matters, including work ethic. He could have chosen to only address the big issues, you know, the "hot topics" like sex, drugs, and alcohol. Instead, he not only tells us what the new life in Christ should look like, but he also models it. The matter at hand today is that of honest, hard work. Similar to our current times, there were people in Paul's day who wanted to benefit from the labor of others without contributing. We call them free-loaders today, but whatever the title we give to it, God calls it theft, dishonest, and ultimately, sin.

I've asked myself countless times what it looks like to be in this world but not of it. James 4:4 tells us that friendship with the world is enmity with God. How then are we to be in the world but not of it? It all comes down to how we live our lives and how we represent Jesus Christ in doing so. Because we have a tendency to focus on the majors or the "big sins," I also believe that we then have a tendency to minimize what we deem as smaller, insignificant issues. The problem with this mentality is that there is a world of people watching our every move. They see when we cut corners to get ahead. They look for integrity in our work, and they determine who Christ is based on what they see in us. When we offer anything less than our best on the job, whatever that "job" may be, we are being dishonest and stealing.

That is what Paul is referencing when he calls us to "honest work." Anything less than honest work is not fitting in the life of the believer.

Our honest, hard work is not only meant to reflect an accurate representation of Jesus to others, but it's also for the benefit of those who are in need. Honest, hard work produces good results. It enables one to provide for oneself as well as one's family, but it also gives one the ability to provide for others who have a need. One of the greatest blessings that my husband and I have been able to share in is the giving of our resources to meet the needs of others. We know several single moms who have very real financial struggles, and there have been many times that we've been able to help. While there are many needs that we aren't able to meet, we do our best to be aware of the ones that we can.

The new life in Christ is marked by honesty and integrity in work ethic, and generosity of what has been given to us. Not only should we be known for honest, hard work, but in addition to that, we should be known for our continual pursuit of helping those who are in need. Are we? Are you? Does integrity characterize your time on the job? Does generosity characterize the stewardship of your resources? It should. The new life in Christ is marked by these things. We have been called to a higher standard. We have been commanded to represent Jesus well. Don't forget that we have an audience.

WEEK SEVEN

DAY 3
TIME FOR REFLECTION

1. I love a teacher who not only tells me to do what is good and best, but one who also models the behavior that they are asking of me. Paul is one such teacher. Read Acts 20:33-35. What does Paul tell us here about his own work ethic?

2. In 1 Thessalonians 4:9-12, Paul commends the church there for how well they are loving other believers. In verse 11, he urges them to do three things. What are they?

3. Read Colossians 3:23-24 and write out these verses below. Is it difficult to maintain this mentality? Why or why not?

DAY 4
THE COST OF DESTRUCTIVE SPEECH

> *"Let no corrupting talk come out of your mouths, but only such as is good for building up, as fits the occasion, that it may give grace to those who hear. And do not grieve the Holy Spirit of God, by whom you were sealed for the day of redemption."* EPHESIANS 4:29-30

Oftentimes with youth comes naiveté. Little thought of consequence has increased the popularity of the expression, "YOLO" (you only live once), and instead of believing that this means living life to the fullest every day, the pursuit has become one of trying to justify the crazy things done. Because "you only live once," right? The caution to heed in this is that when there is little thought to the cost of our actions, there is a tendency toward increased immoral living.

The first instruction we are given in our passage today has to do with the tongue and what we allow to pass over our lips. The word "corrupting" in verse 29 literally means unwholesome, and it refers to that which is foul or rotten. Both of those words induce a memory in my sense of smell. I live in a neighborhood where our trash is picked up once a week. Being that it is only my husband and I accumulating trash in our home, a once a week pick up is typically more than enough. The problem arose one summer when we missed our pick-up date...two weeks in a row. For those of you who don't know, I live in Arizona, also known as the land of the unrelenting sun. It's more than just hot here during the summer months, and in the kind of heat we have here, it takes a matter of minutes for garbage to start producing a very foul odor. This garbage had been sitting in our can outside for three weeks, baking in temperatures that were well over 100 degrees. "Foul" and "rotten" hardly describe the smells that were coming from that can when we finally hauled it out to the curb. Because the can sits outside, we had the luxury of rarely needing to deal with the smell. So, it festered. Then, we stepped outside, and the assault of the smell alone was more consequence than we would ever need to learn our lesson, once and for all.

This is the picture Paul is trying to paint in our minds when it comes to our speech. Any corrupting or unwholesome talk that comes out of our mouths spoils everyone within earshot and has the capacity to rot the hearts and the minds of the hearers. Gossip, slander, foul language, murmuring and complaining, fits of rage—they all corrupt and are unwholesome, completely unfitting speech for the child of God. As yeast spreads through the dough and cannot be removed once it has been added, so are our words. Once our thoughts have materialized into words, they can never be taken back. They either bless or curse. They either give life or produce death. They either build up or tear down. As believers who represent Jesus Christ, our speech should be instructive, encouraging, and uplifting—always. There is a high cost for our destructive speech. When we allow our mouths to run faster than our feet, there is a price to be paid.

Ephesians 4:30 does more than hint at the cost of our destructive speech. It lays it out clearly for all to see. Are you ready for this?

Our destructive speech grieves the Holy Spirit of God.

I want you to take a moment right now to reflect on the last time you grieved. When was the last time your heart ached, your shoulders shook with sobs, your tears endlessly streamed? Grief is a strong word. Mental suffering or distress is something that many of us would rather avoid in life if we could. Know this: when we as the redeemed refuse to change our old ways of sin that characterized our lives before Christ, including our speech, the heart of God is grieved. Our speech should be significantly different than it was prior to us meeting Jesus at the foot of His cross. Is gossip an easy and natural default for you? Are you quick to speak but slow to listen? Are your words charged with malice and anger? When you're upset or angry, does foul language readily flow from your lips?

As much as we might prefer to minimize this area of sin, God certainly does not. If our speech can grieve the heart of God, it should also grieve our own hearts. The cost is too high for us to willfully continue down this destructive path. Not only can our words injure those who hear them, but more importantly, our sinful words grieve God. Let this be more than enough reason to "let no corrupting talk come out of your mouths." Choose to bless with your words instead. Choose to give grace with your speech. Choose to live a life that not only is consistent with your calling to new life, but one that pleases the Holy Spirit of God.

WEEK SEVEN

DAY 4
TIME FOR REFLECTION

1. The book of Proverbs is full of wisdom, including wisdom for our words. Read Proverbs 15:23, 24:26, and 25:11 and write out each verse below.

2. Read Psalm 141:3. Use this verse and the space below to write your own prayer to the Lord, asking Him to help your speech to be filled with grace and truth.

3. One of my favorite verses in the book of Psalms is Psalm 19:14. I have adopted this verse as a significant part of my prayer life. What does it say? In what ways has God shown you today that your words have not been pleasing and acceptable in His sight?

4. The primary purpose of our mouths is to bring God glory, and secondly, to bless others. If you have a concordance at the end of your Bible, look up the word *praise*. There should be several Scripture references that use this one word. Look up each verse. Pick two of the verses you find, write them out below, and commit to putting them into practice this week.

DAY 5
REPLACING DAMAGING EMOTIONS WITH FORGIVENESS

 "Let all bitterness and wrath and anger and clamor and slander be put away from you, along with all malice. Be kind to one another, tenderhearted, forgiving one another, as God in Christ forgave you." EPHESIANS 4:31-32

When it comes to the matter of forgiveness, you and I will never be without opportunity to practice this obedience. People will hurt us, offend us, disappoint us, and betray us, and when they do, will we be found walking our talk? When they do, will we be found having a conviction about forgiveness? Will we be found extending forgiveness, just as forgiveness has been extended to us? Or will we allow bitterness to take root in our hearts, beginning a downward spiral of damaging emotions? It will be one or the other. Where will we be found?

I want to begin today by building on the foundation we laid yesterday: the cost of destructive speech. First, I will submit to you today that a root of destructive speech is unforgiveness. Notice, I did not say "the" root but rather "a" root. If destructive speech in any of its forms is a part of your life, it is fair to say that you may have an unforgiveness issue. If gossip comes easily to you, you may have an unforgiveness issue. If your words are commonly laced with anger or bitterness, you may have an unforgiveness issue. In Matthew 12:34, Jesus, Himself, tells us that our words come from the overflow of our hearts, meaning that what is in our hearts eventually comes out of our mouths. Our words matter, and our words are telling.

The second truth that I want to share with you today regarding the issue of unforgiveness in our lives is this: Unforgiveness produces damaging emotions. Notice the downward spiral of emotions that is listed in Ephesians 4:31: bitterness, wrath, anger, clamor, slander, and malice. The longer we allow ourselves to hold onto the offense, the more unforgiveness festers in our hearts. The longer unforgiveness festers in our hearts, the further down this spiral we fall. Like a coal from the fire in your hand is unforgiveness to your soul. The longer you hold on to it, the more it hurts you.

We see in Ephesians 4:31 that it starts with bitterness, which is essentially a smoldering resentment. Bitterness is the mark of the person who refuses reconciliation. It is the record of wrongs written on the heart. What a lemon is to your mouth, bitterness is to your soul. If not dealt with, bitterness leads to wrath, which is a deeply settled anger that is often violent or eruptive. When not dealt with, wrath and anger lead to clamor, which is the noise of relational strife. Clamor is the mark of the angry person who requires everyone to hear their grievance. When not dealt with, clamor leads to slander, which is the depth of evil speech. These are words that are intended to injure, and these are words that are in no way fitting for a child of God. When not dealt with, slander leads to malice, which is ultimately a bad-heartedness. This is the root of all vices. Now stop and think about this for just a minute. It starts with an offense. If not dealt with, it can lead all the way down the spiral to malice.

How do we stop this downward spiral of damaging emotions? How can we avoid a life of unforgiveness? The key to finding freedom from unforgiveness is choosing to remember how much God has forgiven you. This is exactly what Ephesians 4:32 is saying. Forgive just as freely as God has forgiven you. In the face of every offense, we have a choice. In the moment of every betrayal, we have a choice. We can choose bitterness, which as we've seen today leads us nowhere worth going. Or we can choose forgiveness. I'm not suggesting to you that it's an easy choice. I'm telling you that it's possible to take the high road. Forgiveness is an act of the will. We can choose it or refuse it. The choice is yours, my friends.

WEEK SEVEN

DAY 5
TIME FOR REFLECTION

1. Forgiveness is a non-negotiable area of obedience. It also happens to be a very difficult obedience. Our motivation to forgive must stem from the forgiveness we have received. Read Micah 7:18 and write it out below.

2. One of my favorite verses on forgiveness is 1 John 1:9. It reveals God's heart of compassion for sinful mankind. Read it and write it out below.

3. There are some verses in Scripture that are much harder for me to swallow. Matthew 6:15 is one of them. What does it say?

4. Who do you need to forgive today? What offense have you been carrying around that is leading you down the spiral of damaging emotions? Journal a prayer of repentance below, asking God to give you the grace and strength to forgive who you need to forgive.

week eight
THE GREATEST LOVE

TEACHING OUTLINE

WEEK 8
THE GREATEST LOVE

EPHESIANS 5:1-2

1. God's greatest commandment is to _____. (verses 1-2)

2. To _____ God is to _____ His commands.

3. How are we to imitate God?
    1. _____ where Jesus _____.
    2. _____ what Jesus _____.
    3. _____ like Jesus _____.

If you have committed to write out the book of Ephesians, take a few minutes right now to write Ephesians 5:1-2 in the back of your workbook.

DAY 1
AN INTOLERANCE FOR TOLERANCE

"But sexual immorality and all impurity or covetousness must not even be named among you, as is proper among saints. Let there be no filthiness nor foolish talk nor crude joking, which are out of place, but instead let there be thanksgiving. For you may be sure of this, that everyone who is sexually immoral or impure, or who is covetous (that is, an idolater), has no inheritance in the kingdom of Christ and God."

EPHESIANS 5:3-5

There is something that I've noticed in my own life as it relates to my walk with Christ. Any extended amount of time spent away from God's Word or His presence results in a numbing of my personal convictions. When I am consistently found in the Word, filling my mind, heart, and soul with truth, my convictions are sharp as a razor, and I find it extremely difficult to slip into old patterns of behavior or thinking. When I allow much time to lapse between encounters with God in His Word, the clear line drawn in the sand between right and wrong becomes increasingly difficult to discern. This is why we were never intended to spend much time apart from the Lord and the instruction in His Word because we are weak and prone to wander. It doesn't take much for our affections to stray from our first love. I'm reminded again and again how painfully human I am.

Through the inspiration of the Holy Spirit, Paul charges the church of Ephesus to steer clear of even a hint of sexual immorality and impurity, knowing that even the slightest taste of this would quickly corrupt and destroy the whole. In the event that they would be tempted to understand this as a warning only against the physical act of sexual sin, Paul elaborates on this even further in saying that this also pertains to their words—our words. While the world indulges in every kind of activity that would bring pleasure, we are called to a much higher standard. The list of sinful behavior and speech described in these few verses characterizes the lives of those who will have "no inheritance in the Kingdom of Christ and God." Sexual immorality, all impurity, covetousness, filthiness, foolish talk, crude joking, idolatry...all are unfitting for a follower of Christ, all are out of place, and all result in no inheritance in the Kingdom of God.

Can we just pause for a moment on this claim? While not always easy to swallow, Scripture is always true and never false in its claims. Whenever God draws the dividing line between His own and those who will not inherit His Kingdom, my ears perk up because more than anything else in this life, I want to be found among the faithful. I want to hear His welcome when I finally see my Savior face to face. Therefore, if God says that a consistent pattern of sexual sin, foolish talk, and crude joking will ultimately result in an eternity separated from Him, I'm ready to live my life with some solid convictions in these areas. You too? Good.

For too long, the bride of Christ has excused personal, sinful behavior and justified unholy living. However, God never has nor will He ever tolerate our sin. We shouldn't, either. As believers in Jesus Christ, as children of God who have been given new life, as sons and daughters who have been redeemed from the pits of sin in which we once dwelled, it's time we embrace an intolerance for tolerance, a refusal to tolerate personal sin any longer. Have we forgotten that these very sins are the sins that nailed Jesus to His cross? Have we so quickly forgotten that these sins separate us from intimate communion with God? Have we forgotten that it was God's hatred of sin that forced Him to look away from the blood-stained face of Christ as He hung on that cross? His holiness cannot nor will it ever tolerate our sin.

If we have been redeemed, let us then live as those who have been redeemed. If we have been given new life in Christ, let us then refuse to walk in the ways of the old life any longer! We are not supposed to look like those who don't know Christ. The patterns and behaviors of our lives should look significantly different. Do they? Are we defined by the pursuit of Christ or the pursuit of pleasure? Determine today whom you will serve—the lusts of the flesh or Jesus Christ. You cannot serve both. Choose to be intolerant of tolerance. Refuse to tolerate personal sin any longer. Rise up, church. Assume your rightful place and start representing Christ well.

WEEK EIGHT

DAY 1
TIME FOR REFLECTION

1   Read Colossians 3:5 and write it out below. What does Colossians 3:6 tell us is coming as a result of these sins?

2   Ephesians 5:4 lists three sins of the tongue. List them below. In contrast to these sins, with what are we commanded to fill our mouths instead?

3   Read Romans 1:18-32. Much is said in this passage about those who continue to walk in sin. Verse 21 seems to be the turning point. What does it say? What is the outcome for those who do not honor God and His ways or give thanks to Him?

4   Has the Lord convicted you today of any area of personal sin in your life that you have tolerated and justified? Using the space below, write a prayer of confession and repentance, choosing today to walk in righteousness.

DAY 2
FROM DARKNESS TO LIGHT

> *"Let no one deceive you with empty words, for because of these things the wrath of God comes upon the sons of disobedience. Therefore do not associate with them; for at one time you were darkness, but now you are light in the Lord. Walk as children of light (for the fruit of light is found in all that is good and right and true), and try to discern what is pleasing to the Lord."*
>
> EPHESIANS 5:6-10

Have you ever found yourself telling someone what you believe they want to hear as opposed to what they need to hear? I think we all have done this at one time or another, but whatever our reasons are for doing so, it is never beneficial to deceive. Withholding the truth, even for the sake of not offending someone, is deception. If I'm being honest, there are certainly situations when I'm tempted to do this. Here's my confession: I tend to be a people pleaser. The sin in this is that I often default to trying to please a person over trying to please God. What does this look like? God asks me to do something, and instead, I do something else in order to gain praise, approval, or acceptance from someone. He tells me to go right, and I turn left. He asks me to serve in one area, and I serve in another. He tells me to speak the truth, and instead, I cower in fear while sugarcoating the truth so as not to offend. As much as I'd like to claim that I don't, unfortunately, I am guilty of this from time to time.

This is what Paul is addressing here in verse six. It is not only deceptive, but it is also extremely unloving to give a false assurance of salvation to someone who professes faith in Christ while living their lives in such a way as is described in Ephesians 5:3-5—in constant pursuit of sin without remorse. The last thing an unrepentant sinner needs is a pat on the back, telling them that they are doing just fine, when in reality, they are running fast in the opposite direction of Jesus. It's another form of people pleasing. One of the hardest things about speaking the truth is that it isn't always the most palatable to those on the receiving end. Translation? Sometimes, the truth hurts, but that doesn't mean that we need to hear it any less. Deception and unholy living are marks of our former way of life before we knew Christ. When we were living in darkness, this type of behavior would be expected. However, we have been called out of darkness and into light. Therefore, we are to walk as children of light.

You and I are being called to take a stand against sin today. When Paul says, "Let no one deceive you with empty words," we must then understand that the sinful behaviors of our former life are neither permissible for the believer nor are they fitting, regardless of what popular opinion preaches. Sin festers in the darkness, which is exactly why it prefers to hide there. It is the light, however, that exposes what resides in the dark. We were once darkness, wallowing in our sinful ways, but now we are light. And if we are light, we should behave as such, being marked by goodness, pursuing righteousness, and walking in truth and integrity. This is the path of obedience that we are called to walk.

One of the many beautiful truths that we repeatedly find within God's Word is that His commands are always coupled with promises. When we walk in this obedience (command), we produce good fruit (promise). Goodness, righteousness, and truth are direct results of walking as children of light, but it doesn't stop there. The more we walk in the light of God's truth, we will have an increased awareness and discernment of what pleases the Lord. The more we know what pleases the Lord, the more we will strive to please Him instead of others. These are the benefits of being children of light. We are no longer bound by the darkness, incapable of seeing or knowing what is good and pleasing to the Lord. The darkness of our pasts has been exposed by the light, and we have been set free. The veil has been removed from our eyes. Do not be deceived any longer. The standard for holy, righteous living has been made known and is clear. Walk as children of the light. Blessing is found in its glow.

WEEK EIGHT

DAY 2
TIME FOR REFLECTION

1. Let's revisit Romans 1:18 today. This verse tells us that God's wrath will come against ungodliness and unrighteousness. What does the final phrase of this verse say? In what ways do we as Christians "suppress the truth?"

2. Read John 3:19-21. What does verse 20 tell us is the motivation of those who prefer the darkness as opposed to the light?

3. One of the benefits of genuine repentance is being relocated from darkness to light. Read 1 John 1:5-10. Verse 7 lists two more benefits that we receive when we choose to walk in the light. What are they?

4. As we continue to walk in the light, our ability to discern God's will develops and grows. The longer we choose to remain in darkness, the harder our hearts become toward the ways and Word of God. How have you seen this to be true in your own life? Romans 12:2 puts it well. Read it and write it out below.

DAY 3
AWAKE O SLEEPER

 "Take no part in the unfruitful works of darkness, but instead expose them. For it is shameful even to speak of the things that they do in secret. But when anything is exposed by the light, it becomes visible, for anything that becomes visible is light. Therefore it says, 'Awake, O sleeper, and arise from the dead, and Christ will shine on you.'"

EPHESIANS 5:11-14

It seems as if I've been waiting over a year to write today's lesson for you, the namesake of this Bible study. Every hour of study, prayer, and writing has led up to this point in our study together today. It was a few years ago when I knew that the Lord was calling me to the book of Ephesians. I remember it like it was yesterday. Driving through the hot desert of Arizona into Southern California, it hit me, as clear as one bug after another smashing into my windshield that day as I drove. Just as Paul wrote to the church in Ephesus, reminding them of sound doctrine and desiring to see them live it out in their lives, I, too, felt compelled to pour every fiber of my being into teaching the truths of his words to each one of you—exposing Biblical poverty in the church and sending out a call for Biblical literacy and Biblical living.

Since that very moment when the divine seemed to collide with my mundane that day, my thoughts, emotions, and energy have been arrested by the message of this book. I feel as if I've breathed, slept, and eaten the words of Ephesians again and again for what seems like a very long time now, and today finally brings you and me to the peak of this mountain. More than anything, I want to be found faithful by my Jesus one day. I want you to be found faithful. I want us to bring along as many as we possibly can into that fold of faithfulness. I want to see the church in my generation rise up and stand up for what we believe, and just as Paul sent out a wake up call to the Ephesians, I desire for us to be a part of a great awakening of souls in our own day, an awakening that the Lord is waiting to see take place.

Paul continues his teaching in these verses today on the importance of being set apart. Our calling as believers is to one of holiness, to be set apart from the world in which we live. Not only are we to refrain from the sinful ways of this world and live righteously before all, we are also to expose the darkness whenever and wherever we see it, especially when it is found within the church. Somewhere along the road in this morally bankrupt world, we, even as believers, have somehow become desensitized to the effects that the darkness can have on us. We try to walk the fence far too often, with one foot in the world and the other in the church. We attempt to get as close to the edge as possible and as near to the fire as we can without falling and without getting burned.

The problem with this mentality is that it is in direct violation of God's commands to us in His Word. On all accounts, we are told to flee from temptation, not to try and overcome it with willpower and sheer determination. This is exactly why the bar is raised for us here in Ephesians 5 with the added instruction to not even speak of the disgraceful things that are done in the darkness. Why? Because even talking about them can be corruptive, to us, individually, and to those with whom we discuss them. Because the Lord knows that we're weak in our flesh, He builds these moral fences for us. In His divine mercy, He gives us boundaries. Because of His deep love for us, He will at times tell us no.

There is beautiful imagery used here with this idea of light, though. Whenever a light is turned on, everything that the light reaches is illuminated. Whatever the darkness concealed before is now exposed by the power of the light. If we walk in the light as we are called to, we bring the light to a dark world, exposing the evil and bringing new life to wherever our feet tread. We bring the hope of salvation to a world that is lost in hopelessness. We bring truth that sets free those held in captivity by all of the lies they have believed. If we are in Christ, we must rise!

WEEK EIGHT

Ephesians 5:14 is the verse that leaps off of the page and pierces my heart. If you and I have tasted and seen that the Lord is truly good, if we have embraced salvation and if we know redemption, and if we have been set free by the love of Jesus Christ, how can we not desire that all would come to know this very light, to drink from this well, and to embrace this love? This is the invitation that verse 14 presents—an invitation to come and drink from the living water, an invitation to leave behind the darkness of the past and walk in the light. It's an invitation to Jesus.

Paul shouts through these words that he penned thousands of years ago, and their echo still reaches us today. Wake up! Rise up! Walk on! To all who believe, hear this today: Know what you believe, and may it be based on the truth of God's Word. Live like you believe it so that those who don't believe will be given reason to believe.

To those who for whatever reason have kept their distance from this light: It's not too late. Your chance hasn't passed you by. Not yet. Salvation is extended to you today. Reach out and grasp it. Cling to it. Receive it.

And to all who already have: Walk in it, my friends. A sleeping church is the last thing this world needs. "Awake, O sleeper!" Let us assume our rightful position within the body of Christ, and His light will shine on us for all to see.

WEEK EIGHT

DAY 3
TIME FOR REFLECTION

1. The command we've been given here is clear: Do not participate in sin of any kind. Read Romans 13:11-14. Verse 14 tells us to make no provision for what? What does this mean?

2. Paul referenced Isaiah 60:1 when he wrote Ephesians 5:14. Read Isaiah 60:1 and write it out below.

3. We read about two other invitations to salvation in Isaiah 55:1-3 and in James 4:6-10. From these two passages, list the benefits that we receive through salvation.

4. The call to "awake" and "arise" has truly convicted me to my core. In what ways is God calling you to "awake" and "arise" today?

DAY 4
A WISE WALK

 "Look carefully then how you walk, not as unwise but as wise, making the best use of the time, because the days are evil. Therefore do not be foolish, but understand what the will of the Lord is."

EPHESIANS 5:15-17

May I have a moment of pure vulnerability with you? Get ready, because I'm about to gush. First, I must tell you what an honor it has been to serve you through this study of Ephesians, and we haven't even finished yet. Teaching God's Word is a calling that I do not take lightly, and I am beyond grateful and thoroughly humbled by the task. Some of you have walked with the Lord longer than I have walked this earth. You all are my heroes of the faith. I glean from you, and I'm so thankful for your whole-hearted, steadfast devotion to our Lord and the example that you set for the rest of us coming up behind you. Others of you are all together new to Bible study, and you must know that it brings my heart such great joy to meet together on the pages of His Word each day. Although we don't get to sit across from one another at a Starbucks table or a kitchen table or a Bible study table, know that I love you, and I dream about the day when we will all worship Jesus together face-to-face.

As much as I've been overjoyed to journey through Paul's writings with you, I've been tremendously convicted along the way. I find it increasingly difficult to look at any given verse in Scripture and not walk away challenged by it or changed because of it. Every day of this study and every moment spent writing it has left me challenged and all together wrecked for more of Jesus, and I pray it will ultimately leave me changed. My honest confession to you today is that wisdom doesn't always describe and define my daily walk, but I pray that one day, it consistently will. There are moments when emotion gets the best of me. There are days when complacency wins. There are times when faithfulness is not my default. Even so, God has somehow called me to this task for such a time as this. To say that I am humbled is an understatement. I can hardly believe that He would work through my mess. I can scarcely understand why He would use my efforts for His glory, but I am grateful that He does. I am thankful that He will continue to, and I come to the table today just as broken and in need of His grace as you, but I come hungry for more of Him. Am I in good company?

The longer I walk with Jesus, the more I understand the weight of influence I can have on others. How I live my life, based on the faith claims that I make, can determine how others will see and interpret Jesus. If I don't walk wisely, my sinful steps can and will cause others to trip and fall. This is why we are given a warning here in Ephesians 5:15 to be careful how we walk because our time is short, the days are evil, and our ability to influence is far greater than we realize.

Therefore, we must ask ourselves this question: "What does a wise walk look like?" Perhaps, we can start by defining what it doesn't look like. The foolish or unwise person isn't named so because of an intellectual limit or void. Rather, foolishness is defined by one who says there is no God and lives their life accordingly. Take a moment to read Psalm 14:1 and write it out on the next page.

The end result for the faithless is a corrupt life marked by sinful deeds. We can then determine that a wise walk begins with faith in Jesus Christ. To live a life based on belief in God and in His Word is to live a wise life. Anything short of this is foolishness. Do you desire a wise walk? Do you want to be characterized by foolishness or by wisdom? A wise walk starts with belief.

Secondly, a wise walk is marked by righteous living. Genuine belief in Christ will always propel the believer toward sanctification. A life that has been saved by grace will ultimately be changed by grace. The foolish or unwise person will continue to default to gratifying the sinful desires of the flesh. The wise person will default to falling in step with the Spirit. A wise walk is full of the fruit of the Spirit. A wise walk starts with belief, and it leads to righteous living.

Finally, a wise walk is marked by intentionality and purpose. The foolish or unwise person will waste his days, but the wise person will seek to make the most of them and to maximize every opportunity given to him. This one life that we've been given is so painfully short. It will be gone before we know it. What are we doing with our time? Are we wasting our lives or are we intentionally and purposefully making the most of our days, seeking to bring God glory in each and every moment that we are given? A wise walk is one of intention and purpose, constantly seeking to bring God glory. A wise walk is a life not wasted.

How then is this accomplished? A wise walk is achieved by the diligent pursuit of knowing God and making Him known. Wisdom and instruction are found in His Word. Are you reading it? Do you study it? How often do you meditate on it? Have you memorized any part of it? Do you share what you've learned with others? We become wise by immersing ourselves in wisdom. God's Word is that wisdom. His Word gives us all that we need to walk wisely. I pray that we will be found wise. I pray that you and I will in unison pursue God through His Word. I pray that you and I will walk wisely.

WEEK EIGHT

DAY 4
TIME FOR REFLECTION

1. The book of Proverbs has a lot to say about foolishness. Read each of the verses below. What do they say about the fool?
   - Proverbs 10:23
   - Proverbs 12:15-16
   - Proverbs 14:16
   - Proverbs 15:5, 14, 21
   - Proverbs 18:2
   - Proverbs 20:3
   - Proverbs 23:9
   - Proverbs 28:26
   - Proverbs 29:11

2. A wise walk is marked by righteous living. Read Galatians 5:22-23 and list below the fruit of the Spirit.

3. A wise walk is a life not wasted, a life filled with intentionality and purpose. Read Colossians 4:2-6. In what ways does this passage specifically instruct us to make the most of our time?

DAY 5
UNDER THE INFLUENCE

> *"And do not get drunk with wine, for that is debauchery, but be filled with the Spirit, addressing one another in psalms and hymns and spiritual songs, singing and making melody to the Lord with all your heart, giving thanks always and for everything to God the Father in the name of our Lord Jesus Christ, submitting to one another out of reverence for Christ."*
>
> EPHESIANS 5:18-21

I recently watched an episode of a teenage drama that was a fairly popular television series when I was in high school. Not an incredibly proud moment for me, I admit, but nonetheless, I walked away with a very clear picture of where I want to take us today in this lesson. Two of the main characters in this show got drunk, and their subsequent behavior was nothing short of what you would expect. They made fools of themselves in front of their family and friends, said things that they completely regretted, and ended the evening worshiping the porcelain goddess, if you know what I mean.

Perhaps, you can relate to this unfortunate scene, remembering the folly of your own youth and the poor decisions you may have made when under the influence. While my intention today is not to induce any kind of shame or guilt, when I saw the above scene unfold, it made me think. When we are under the influence of such a substance, we will say and do things that we normally would not. No doubt, this is why God gives us clear instruction in His Word against drunkenness. On the contrary, He tells us that the only thing we should be "filled" with is the Spirit. Instead of allowing ourselves to be filled with alcohol, drugs, or any other substance that would control us under its influence, we are commanded to be continually be under the influence of the Spirit, because it is only under His influence that our lives will be pleasing to the Lord.

The phrase "be filled with the Spirit" in verse 18 is not referring to the Spirit's indwelling or even baptism by the Spirit, because every Christian is indwelt by the Spirit at the moment of salvation. What Paul is telling us here is to consistently live our lives under the influence of the Spirit by allowing God's Word to control us and its truth to determine our course. What exactly would this look like for the believer? A pursuit of righteous and pure living, a posture of repentance over all known sin, a dying to self and its desires, a surrender to God's will, and a full reliance on Christ's power in all things. This is what it would look like to consistently live under the influence of the Spirit.

If we were to position ourselves under this influence, we would say and do things that we normally would not. We would forgive when the wounds seem too deep to ever heal. We would love in the face of hate. We would be patient and kind even though we live in a world that isn't. We would speak the truth and be honest even when society tells us to exaggerate to cover our tracks or to cut corners to get ahead. We would know the joy of the Lord, and it would gush from our veins and pour out through our words, even in the midst of heartache, disappointment, frustration, or despair.

If we would live our lives under the influence of the Spirit, the immediate personal consequences that we would know are listed for us in Ephesians 5:19-21. We would sing songs. We would give thanks. We would humbly and willingly submit to one another in Christ. Can you fathom what a different place this world would be? Can you even comprehend what the church would look like? Imagine: the body of Christ rejoicing; His bride being thankful; the church being humble; believers being reverent. This is what the church could be.

Breathe that in for just a moment. Ponder this. A life lived under the influence of the Spirit is the life that we are all called to. There is not one exception. To position yourself under the control and leading of God, His Spirit, and His Word is to walk in obedience to this command. I long for the day when the church as a whole awakens to this call and rises to this obedience. I am eager to see the day when every follower of Christ desires to live in the conscious presence of Jesus Christ, allowing our minds and our hearts to be dominated by God's Word in all things. I want to be filled with the Spirit. I want to live under the influence.

WEEK EIGHT

DAY 5
TIME FOR REFLECTION

1. This call to new life in Christ seems to be somewhat repetitive in Paul's writing. In several different ways throughout the book of Ephesians, he reminds his readers of the new life in Christ in which we are to walk. His peers were also very passionate about this as well. I love how Peter puts it in 1 Peter 4:2-3. Read this verse and write it out below.

2. Living under the influence of the Spirit results in certain behavior. Ephesians 5:19-21 is not the only place in Scripture that tells us what this looks like. Read Colossians 3:16. When we allow God's Word to dwell in us, what is the result according to this verse?

3. Let's practice living under the influence of the Spirit together, right now. This influenced life results in singing, thanksgiving, and humility. Below, list one or two of your favorite worship songs. Write out a few of the lyrics that bless you the most. Make a list of ten things that you are thankful for today. Then, read Philippians 2:3 and write it out below. Choose today to live your life under the influence of the Spirit.

week nine
SUBMISSION IS NOT A DIRTY WORD

TEACHING OUTLINE

WEEK 9
SUBMISSION IS NOT A DIRTY WORD

EPHESIANS 5:22-33

1 Submission is our _____ unto the Lord. (verses 22-24)

2 Submission is God's _____ of _____ for His daughters. (verses 25-33)

3 Submission is not:

4 Submission is an _____ of voluntary _____; a _____ to willingly place oneself under another's authority.

> If you have committed to write out the book of Ephesians, take a few minutes right now to write Ephesians 5:22-33 in the back of your workbook.

DAY 1
THE 1ST COMMANDMENT WITH A PROMISE

 "Children, obey your parents in the Lord, for this is right. Honor your father and mother (this is the first commandment with a promise), that it may go well with you and that you may live long in the land."

EPHESIANS 6:1-3

At this point in our study together, I feel as if we have become friends. Whether we ever meet on this side of heaven or not, we have walked through the pages of Ephesians together, and this journey will be one that I will never forget. I don't know about you, but I open up to my friends. I tell them the details of my life, and I choose to be transparent with them because that is what friendship is all about. I consider you friends. So, here goes. I was quite the rebellious child. No, really, I was. While my younger sister was the obedient one who never seemed to push boundaries, I was the one who always challenged authority. Some of the first words I remember hearing from my parents were "no" and "obey."

Throughout my childhood years and even into adolescence, I had a rebellious streak in me. Obedience seemed to be a dirty word, one that I was not fond of. I wanted to do what I wanted to do when I wanted to do it. Anybody? While I'd like to say that I've grown out of those old, sinful patterns, the reality is that I still struggle with this today. Obedience is hard for me. I don't like rules. I tend to demand the "why" behind the "what" of most things, and although our passage of Scripture today is speaking of obedience in the context of the child/parent relationship, obedience is a life-long principle that you and I are to embrace.

Even though obedience has always been a rather difficult thing for me, I have to admit that I'm grateful that God gives us this instruction and asks us to start walking in this from the time of childhood. The patterns that we establish in youth are most often the ones that remain throughout our lives. God knows this about us. He understands that we are painfully human, and He desires that we start young in our pursuit of righteous living. Therefore, in His love, He gently calls out to us as children, "My child, obey the parents that I've placed over you. It's for your good. You will be blessed. Trust me in this."

The heart of this command to live our lives in obedience is not for God to give us a mile-long list of dos and don'ts. No, His heart in this is for everything that we do to be done as if unto the Lord. As children, when we are instructed to obey our parents, it is because our obedience to them is honoring to the Lord. Even from the young ages of childhood, we can begin patterns of honoring and glorifying the Lord through our obedience. Imagine that. At the tender age of 5, we have the capacity to make God smile. We have the ability to bless His heart, and the more that we forge these roads of obedience in our lives, the more likely we are to default to obedience in the future.

Is obedience a consistent pattern in your life? Do you choose to submit yourself under the authorities that God has placed over you? Do both your words and actions reflect a heart of obedience? Is obedience as hard for you as it has been for me? The more I've studied God's Word, the more I've come to understand this eternal truth:

God blesses obedience.

Every time, without fail, His promises are true. What He says He will do, He will do. The command to obey our parents and to establish patterns of obedience to authority in our lives comes linked to a very precious promise. The promise that awaits those who embrace this command is the blessing of a long life and a good life. Long and good, of course, is according to God's economy, but nevertheless, long and good. Again, this comes down to an accurate understanding of God's ways. He will always bless obedience, and we will always be recipients of those blessings if we choose to walk in obedience. Always. I am so grateful for a God who not only commands, but for One who promises and blesses.

WEEK NINE

DAY 1
TIME FOR REFLECTION

1. Paul is citing a passage from the Old Testament here, one that I imagine you might be familiar with. Read Exodus 20:1-17 and write out verse 12 below.

2. Obedience is such an integral part of our walk that God made certain to include this command throughout Scripture. Read Proverbs 6:20-23. What are the benefits listed in these verses of our willingness to obey?

3. Jesus raised the bar for us in regard to obedience when He spoke the words from John 15:14. In your own words, what does this verse say?

4. Using the space below, journal a prayer of confession, asking God to reveal to you any area of rebellion that is present in your life, repent of it, and commit to walking in obedience to all of His commands. Thank Him for His promises that are linked to every command He gives.

DAY 2
PARENTING 101

 "Fathers, do not provoke your children to anger, but bring them up in the discipline and instruction of the Lord." EPHESIANS 6:4

Apparently, this week must be the week for vulnerability and confession on my part. So far, you know that I was a fairly rebellious child from yesterday's lesson. Today, I have another confession to bring to the table. Are you ready for this one?

I'm not a parent.

Some of you might already be thinking, "Um, is that a bad thing, Cherie?" No, of course it's not, but the true confession is really rooted more in my insecurity about this fact. I've been teaching Bible studies and leading women now for several years. I was only twenty-three years old when I taught my first Bible study to a large group of women at my church, and most of the women in attendance were old enough to be my mother. Since I began women's ministry, I've taught mothers and grandmothers—women who are older and have much more life experience than me. Last year, I was asked to speak to a moms group, and for several months leading up to this, I was shaking in my boots. I don't really have a fear of public speaking, but I was so worried that I would be perceived as inadequate or unworthy to take the stage at an event such as this.

My point? I'm coming to you today as a humble servant, preparing to teach a portion of Scripture to you about parenting, and while I am not a parent yet, I pray that God will still speak to your hearts through the wisdom of His Word and the words that He has given me on this topic. Although I do not have biological children, God has allowed me to spiritually mother several, and so I will speak from this experience.

This verse begins by specifically addressing fathers, but since Paul was just speaking of both parents in the previous verses, we can assume that this verse can be applied to both, as well. Also, the word that is translated for "father" here in Ephesians 6:4 is the same word used for "parents" in Hebrews 11:23, so let's move forward in assuming that this instruction is for both mothers and fathers. It was a common reality in Paul's day for fathers to rule their homes with stern and domineering authority. Because women and children were mostly viewed as second-class citizens, their emotional needs and welfare were seldom considered. Love was not the motivating factor of the father role in many cases.

Paul speaks very clearly to this fallout in verse four by saying that this type of parenting is unacceptable for the Christ-following parents. Even though the unbelieving world may live their lives void of a loving and Christ-centered home, Christians should not. While parents have been given the awesome weight of responsibility to raise their children to know and love the Lord, their authority should never be characterized by unreasonable demands that are void of love—demands that will ultimately lead their children to a place of anger, despair, and resentment. While children will seldom enjoy being disciplined, the underlying motivation in parenting should always be love.

What does it look like, then, to discipline children according to God's commands and to raise them under the instruction of the Lord? Like most, if not all things, I believe this is a matter of the heart. Before you discipline your child for doing something wrong, check your own heart. Are you angry and is your response to them one that is filled with rage? Is your discipline coming from an emotional outburst, or is your discipline coming from a place of love? When your children disobey and directly violate the boundaries you have set for them, your heart will hurt. You will be discouraged. You might even be angry, but like any other emotion in life, we must submit ourselves to the Lord first and foremost in all things, including the discipline and instruction of our children. Every teachable moment with your children should be for the purpose of showing them the love of Christ and pointing them toward a righteous walk. Do you parent in love? Are you sowing seeds of love into your children? Does your discipline point them toward God's love? It should.

WEEK NINE

DAY 2
TIME FOR REFLECTION

1. One of my all-time favorite passages on discipline comes from Hebrews 12:5-11. This passage reveals God's heart for us as His children. What does verse 11 teach us will be the end result of enduring under the Lord's discipline?

2. Read Proverbs 13:24 and write it out below. What principle does this verse teach in regard to parenting?

3. I can speak from experience in saying that there are innumerable blessings that have filled my life because of the "discipline and instruction of the Lord" in which my mother raised me. Read 2 Timothy 3:14-15. What specific blessing is listed in verse 15 for those who have allowed this discipline and instruction to change them?

DAY 3
WHEN NO ONE IS WATCHING

 "Slaves, obey your earthly masters with fear and trembling, with a sincere heart, as you would Christ, not by the way of eye-service, as people-pleasers, but as servants of Christ, doing the will of God from the heart..." EPHESIANS 6:5-6

Someone once described integrity to me as having consistent moral character, even when no one is watching. In other words, your public display should also match your private display. What does this look like? You're not only a church attendee on Sundays, but you're a pursuer of God Monday through Saturday. You're honest in your dealings with people. Your private prayer life surpasses your public one. This is what integrity looks like. It is a life lived for the praise and approval of God and not man.

Today's passage is somewhat of a tricky one. The Bible doesn't speak against slavery itself, but rather it speaks against its abuses. Mistreatment and abuse of mankind will always be something that grieves the heart of God. However, since our context for slavery would primarily fall under its sinful expressions, when we read these verses, I imagine we wonder at them. Is God condoning slavery? Does the Bible say it's permissible? Slaves were very common in Biblical times, and they were commonly abused by their owners. Because Paul's audience was very familiar with the presence of slavery, there was a great need for this to be addressed.

My approach to our passage today will not be one of addressing slavery. Instead, I want to speak to the principles that I believe Paul is addressing here: integrity and respect. In order for us to be able to apply this teaching to our lives, let's look at this in regard to the employer/employee relationship. The command to be obedient in verse five literally means to maintain a continuous submission to one's earthly master. For us, this would refer to our boss. Who do you report to? Even if you are the boss, there is some level of accountability that should be above you. Are you obedient to those who have been placed over you in authority? Do you only obey or submit when they are watching?

The matter at hand is respect for authority and integrity in it. I've already confessed that this is a tough one for me; however, we are not off the hook just because this obedience is hard. Scripture doesn't tell us to respect those who deserve respect or those who are respectable. We are told to unequivocally respect those above us in authority. Period. As with the previous teaching on submission from Ephesians 5, God never requires us to submit to authority when it comes to sin, but in every other way, we are to submit to and respect the authority that God has placed over us. The reason we are to respect them is not because they might deserve our respect, but it is because we are to be respecting them "as servants of Christ," or as we would respect and serve Christ Himself. Essentially, Paul is telling us here that to serve your employer with a sincere heart and with respect is to serve the Lord well. This, my friends, is an act of worship.

When it comes to our obedience, God is after our hearts, not our hands. He cares far more about our motivations and intentions than our production or performance. While man looks at the outward appearance and judges based on performance, God looks at the heart. Are you working as unto the Lord in all things? Are you seeking to be honest and full of integrity at work? Do you demonstrate respect for authority, both publicly and privately? Because what you do when no one is watching is who you really are.

WEEK NINE

DAY 3
TIME FOR REFLECTION

1. Paul was pretty clear in his instruction on this matter. Even so, he repeats himself, almost verbatim, in his letter to the Colossians. Read Colossians 3:22 and write it out below.

2. When Samuel was given the task of selecting Israel's next king, David appeared to be the least likely candidate. The youngest of his brothers, not overly impressive in appearance, and a humble shepherd, David probably would not have been my pick at first glance. However, he was God's pick. Read 1 Samuel 16:7. According to this verse, what matters most to God?

3. In what ways do you struggle with integrity? In what ways do you struggle with respecting authority? What do you need to confess to the Lord today?

4. Using the space provided below, journal a prayer of response to the Lord today. Commit to do all things as unto Him, seeking to please Him and striving to live a life of integrity.

DAY 4
GOD STILL SEES

 "...rendering service with a good will as to the Lord and not to man, knowing that whatever good anyone does, this he will receive back from the Lord, whether he is a slave or free." EPHESIANS 6:7-8

We don't have to search too hard or look very far to find that our world is filled with injustice. All you need to do is turn on the nightly news, and you will hear and see more than you'd probably like to. This is a hard life in a hard world. If we, as believers, didn't possess hope in Christ, I don't know how we would make it day to day. Honestly, I don't know how those who don't believe get through each day without this hope. One thing you and I can be confident of is this: God sees all, and one day, He will set all things right. We can bank our lives on this truth. We can possess great hope because of this truth. We can live lives of obedience because of this truth, whether we ever see reward on earth or not.

Paul finishes his instruction and completes his thought to slaves (or employees, from our lesson yesterday) in verses seven and eight. Yesterday, we looked long and hard at the motivation of our hearts—the why behind what we do. I imagine it was as convicting for you as it was for me, and while it may have been a difficult day of homework for you, I pray it was a beneficial one. It is always good to be challenged by God's Word, and it is even better to be changed by it. My prayer is that you have come to today's lesson with renewed conviction and steadfast hope. The God we serve is a God who gives us good reason for every single obedience that He calls us to. Just as we've already stated but cannot say enough, God blesses obedience.

The timeless truth that we are able to grasp from these verses in Ephesians is that God will never allow any good work done for His glory to go unnoticed or unrewarded by Him. People may overlook our efforts and dismiss our good works, but God never will. We can be confident of that. This truth gives us all the more reason to work and live to please God and not man, knowing that our rewards are eternal and will not fade. When the motivation of our hearts is pure, the reward is inevitable. This is the God we serve. He sees all. He knows all. Nothing escapes His knowledge. No obedience goes unnoticed. Ever.

The confidence we can walk in, then, is that God not only sees our good works and will reward us for them if they are done as unto Him, but He also sees our mistreatment. Sin never escapes the watchful eye of God, and all sin bears consequence. You and I can rest in the certainty that justice will come. Any and all abuse or mistreatment that you have endured has not gone unnoticed by our God. All injustice committed against you was seen by a Holy God, and one day God will set all things right. He will right all wrongs. He will judge all sin. And He will bless all obedience.

To those who are desperately trying to be faithful in this hard, cruel world: Keep pressing on, friends. Keep pursuing righteous living. Keep walking in obedience. Keep loving your spouse, even when they seem unlovable. Keep prioritizing time on your knees in prayer and the Word, even when you don't feel like it. Keep loving your enemy and doing good to those who persecute you, even when you feel as if you're losing hope. Keep doing it all for God's approval and for His praise. Reward awaits you. Blessing is just around the corner. God sees your efforts. He sees your good works. Nothing escapes His vision. He has not, nor will He ever overlook you. So, press on. Even when no one is watching and no one recognizes all that you do, do it all as unto the Lord. He still sees.

WEEK NINE

DAY 4
TIME FOR REFLECTION

1. The call to follow Jesus is not an easy road. On the contrary, in order to follow Jesus, we are told that we have to deny ourselves and carry His cross. Read Matthew 16:24-27. What promise are we given in verse 27?

2. Scripture is consistent with these truths: God sees all, and God will judge all, both our righteous and sinful deeds. Read 2 Corinthians 5:10 and write it out below. What hope are you given from this verse?

3. Read Hebrews 4:12-13 and write out verse 13 below.

4. I frequently spend time in the Psalms. They are filled with prayers and praise, and often I will read and re-read a Psalm, over and over again. Psalm 37 is one of my most frequented chapters. The sub-title in my Bible for Psalm 37 says, "He will not forsake His Saints." Read Psalm 37:1-3. We are given two commands in verse one. What are they? What promise are we given in verse two? What four things does verse three tell us that we should do instead?

DAY 5
THE SPIRIT-FILLED BOSS

 "Masters, do the same to them, and stop your threatening, knowing that He who is both their Master and yours is in heaven, and that there is no partiality with Him."

EPHESIANS 6:9

I consider it an incredible privilege to have been born and raised in a Christian home and community. Most of my life has been immersed in the church, to one degree or another. I attended Christian school from Kindergarten through High School graduation. I was able to continue my education in Bible college. After college graduation, I went on to work at a church. For the past several years, I've worked and volunteered for Christians and Christian organizations. The last few years led me to start my own Christian ministry for women called Neue Thing. I've been both the employee and the boss. From start to finish, I have been extremely blessed. Even within some of the corporate or secular jobs I have held, some of my employers were believers. If you have any of these details in common with me, you also know that it is a blessing. To work with or for like-minded people is a gift.

While my story may seem a bit sugar-coated or too good to be true, I assure you, it is not. I'm also fully aware of the fact that many of you don't share my experience in the work field, and perhaps this has made it extremely difficult for you to maintain your morals and beliefs in an unbelieving world. My purpose today is not to determine which end of the spectrum is better than the other; rather, I want to speak to those who find themselves in authority over others and hopefully shed some biblical light on these roles of leadership. If you are a boss or a "master," God has some specific instruction for you today. Will you join me in pursuing truth today, friends? Will you humble yourselves and choose to be teachable? Let's dive in!

In the previous verses of Ephesians 6, Paul gave clear instruction to those who are subject to masters to honor and respect them and to work for them as if working for the Lord Himself. Now, Paul directs his words toward those in authority over others. If you are a believer, your faith in Jesus Christ should be evident in every area of your life, both personally and professionally. It would be inconsistent with the faith you profess to compartmentalize your life and to leave Jesus out of your work and the way you lead. What Paul is teaching in Ephesians 6:5-9 is that there should be a mutual respect between employers and employees, and for believers, this should stem from their love and commitment to Jesus Christ. The servant should humbly serve, and the master should humbly lead.

Therefore, a Christian boss who threatens, abuses, or is even inconsiderate to those under them is a poor example and a horrible representation of Jesus Christ. It is extremely important for us all to remember that anyone who is in a position of power or authority has been placed there by God. He is the one who appoints rulers, not man. Every aspect of earthly authority rests under the sovereign hand of Almighty God. Since this authority has been given to those who possess it, they are to demonstrate their authority with justice, grace, and love. The Spirit-filled boss understands fully that he also has a Master to whom he must give an account, a Heavenly One. Everyone on this earth, no matter how high in authority they sit, answers to God—the President of the United States, the CEOs and the CFOs, the senior pastor of the church, the store manager, the small business owner, and the list could go on. One day, we all will give an account to THE Master, and we will be held to His standard, not our own.

If you are in a position of overseeing others, if you are a boss, supervisor, or a team leader, are you operating in that position of authority under the leadership and instruction of the Holy Spirit? Are you the Spirit-filled boss, the one who leads with justice, grace, and love? Or are you domineering, micro-managing, inconsiderate, and harsh? Are you respected by those under you, or do you demand their respect? Do you give respect to those whom you lead? In your position of authority, do you represent Christ well? Be a "master" who deserves respect, not one who demands it. Lead as Christ led. Follow in the footsteps of the One who was the selfless servant. Be the Spirit-filled boss.

WEEK NINE

DAY 5
TIME FOR REFLECTION

1. The God we serve is a relational God. He exists in relationship with the Son and the Spirit. Therefore, He cares deeply about relationships, even the relationship between the employer and employee. He always has, and He always will. Leviticus 25:43 addresses this principle, as well. Based on this verse, what should the defining characteristic be of the one in authority over another?

2. The Spirit-filled boss is the one who continually seeks to operate under the influence of the Holy Spirit. According to 2 Peter 1:5-8, what virtues should be increasing in the life of the believer? List them below. How can these virtues be expressed in the work place?

3. Ephesians 6:9 ends with a statement about partiality. Because God does not pick and choose His favorites and show special favor to them, the Spirit-filled boss shouldn't either. Read James 2:1 and James 2:9 and write out both verses below.

Week Ten
ARMOR UP!

TEACHING OUTLINE

WEEK 10
ARMOR UP!

EPHESIANS 6:10-13

1 The warning of battle is not intended to _____ us, but rather to _____ us. (verses 10-11)

2 We would do well in remembering that the _____ is our _____. (verse 12)

3 The armor we have been given _____ us to _____ _____ without _____ in the face of the enemy's attacks. (verse 13)

If you have committed to write out the book of Ephesians, take a few minutes right now to write Ephesians 6:10-13 in the back of your workbook.

DAY 1
TRUTH & RIGHTEOUSNESS

 "Stand therefore, having fastened on the belt of truth, and having put on the breastplate of righteousness…"

EPHESIANS 6:14

Friends, today marks the beginning of the final week in our study of the book of Ephesians. My heart is filled with emotion. I can't begin to express the joy that is about to erupt out of my pores just knowing that many of you took a few steps closer to Jesus along the way. In just a few more days, we will be able to say that we have spent ten weeks poring over each word that Paul penned to the church in Ephesus, and I pray we are more like Jesus because of it. I hope we will be able to shout in unison, "Every minute of reading was worth it. Every hour spent in study was a blessing. Every verse memorized was beneficial. Every word was life-giving, thirst-quenching, and soul-reviving." I pray that you have had tender moments with our King. I trust that you have tasted His goodness and been marked by His presence. I believe that you will be forever changed because of this journey through God's Word. Not a moment was wasted. Not a minute was in vain. There is a vast amount of unknown in this life, but one thing we can be certain of is this: Every moment spent in God's Word will be a moment well spent. His Word never returns void!

If the Lord has used this study to awaken even one sleeper, it was all worth it. If God's Word came alive to even one, I would do it all over again and again. To all of you who have made it this far: Thank you for the privilege it has been to lead you along this road and to teach you the priceless truths that the Lord has taught me. I am so grateful for you. I am so thankful for God's Word. I am in awe of the One we are pursuing. You too? Praise God!

I hope we need no reminder that we are engaged in a battle—not a battle of flesh and blood, but a spiritual war that rages in the heavens, a battle for souls. This news should not frighten us, but rather motivate us. If we are in Christ, we stand on the winning side! The battle rages on, but we know the outcome. Jesus Christ is Lord, and He defeated sin and death once and for all on the cross. This life He has entrusted to each one of us is one that is also intended to be victorious. So, how are we to fight this battle? With our armor on. Ephesians 6:14 (NIV) begins with the command to "stand firm," which is the third time this command is written since verse ten, signifying its importance. The pieces of spiritual armor that we will spend the remainder of this week studying are the very things that will be our defense again the devil, his demons, their works, and effects. Every time Satan tempts us to doubt God's Word, to disobey His commands, to live in fear, to dwell in confusion, to cause division, to live hypocritically, to forsake godliness, or to oppose truth, the armor of God is our defense against him and his schemes. This is why it is so critical that we know God's Word, spend time in it, and spend our lives living it.

The two pieces of armor that we will focus on today are the belt of truth and the breastplate of righteousness. It was common for soldiers in ancient times to wear a loose-fitting tunic in battle. Since their combat was primarily hand-to-hand, a loose-fitting garment would serve as a hindrance in the fight, getting in the way of the quick movements required of the soldier. Therefore, the soldier would gather up the loose ends of the garment and tie it together with the belt, thus removing any obstacle that would get in the way of a victorious fight on his part. When it comes to the spiritual battle that we are engaged in, the belt that will tie up all loose ends and ensure that every obstacle has been moved out of our way is truth. Truth exposes error. Truth illuminates falsehood and deception. Truth sets us free. The devoted Christ-follower will seek to remove every obstacle that stands in their way from a victorious end. Truth is our guard.

Finally, we are instructed to put on the breastplate of righteousness. The soldier's breastplate would cover their full torso, thus protecting the heart and other vital organs. Injury in this area would most often result in death. Spiritually speaking, as we walk in obedience to God's Word and His ways, we become more like Christ. As we become more like Christ, we take on His attributes of righteousness and holiness. In Christ, we are covered in His righteousness and holiness. With these characteristics of Christ resting on us as believers, they serve as a safeguard against the enemy. Christ's righteousness is our spiritual breastplate. Without this covering, we remain vulnerable to the attacks of the enemy.

Friend, sojourner, pursuer of Christ:

Put on your belt of truth. Put on your breastplate of righteousness. Stand firm against the enemy. Be victorious in the fight!

WEEK TEN

DAY 1
TIME FOR REFLECTION

1. In order to be victorious in this fight, we must remove every obstacle that would get in our way. If we are to pursue righteous living, every weight that would hinder us in this pursuit must be laid aside. Read Hebrews 12:1-2 and write out these verses below.

2. What are some of your "obstacles" right now, things that get in the way of a whole-hearted, steadfast pursuit of Jesus Christ? What distracts you from a life of full devotion to Him? Pray and ask God to reveal each and every obstacle and list them below.

3. Read Deuteronomy 6:25. According to this verse, what is our righteousness?

4. Without righteousness, we remain vulnerable to our enemy. Since we now know that obedience is linked to righteousness, what is one practical way that you can walk in obedience to God's Word today?

DAY 2
PEACE & FAITH

 "...and, as shoes for your feet, having put on the readiness given by the gospel of peace. In all circumstances take up the shield of faith, with which you can extinguish all the flaming darts of the evil one..." EPHESIANS 6:15-16

Can we all just stop for a moment and pause for the obvious right now? Shoes! I love it! In God's goodness and generosity, He made sure to equip us with some good shoes for our feet. Ladies, don't tell me this doesn't thrill you a bit! At the risk of sounding terribly materialistic, I'll confess that I do love myself some shoes. There, I said it. I do. I love shoes, and so I find it somewhat exciting that God saw fit to provide us with shoes in this battle. While I'd like to imagine that these shoes are somewhat fashionable, more importantly, they are practical.

Let's remember what we're talking about here in Ephesians 6. We are engaged in a spiritual battle, and God has equipped us with all the necessary armor to successfully win this fight. We only need to put it on. The right shoes were just as important in the armor as the rest. Soldiers in Paul's time wore boots with nails in them, allowing them to firmly grip the ground during combat and providing them with stability. This type of shoe gave them the ability to (don't miss this) "stand firm" when the enemy was coming against them. In Christ, we stand on the winning side. We've already addressed this truth. It is so important to remember now, though, because the knowledge of this truth gives us confidence in the fight. This confidence is our ability to "stand firm" and to not be moved by the schemes and attacks of the enemy. With every piece of armor in place, including our shoes of peace, we are guaranteed a victory.

"The gospel of peace" is the good news that all who have come to faith in Jesus Christ as Savior are now at peace with God. Further, because we are now at peace with God, we can be certain that God is our strength in the battle. He fights for us. He fights against our enemy. He defeats our enemy. We have been given divine support, and it is this that enables us to stand firm in the "readiness given by the gospel of peace." This is our protective footwear. The gospel of peace is our anchor and hope.

Now, we've come to the shield. I love this part! A roman shield was typically very large. About two and a half feet wide by four and a half feet tall, the shield served as full-body protection against the onslaught of the enemy. With the shield raised in place, every arrow or spear could be deflected. The shield of faith that we are called to raise refers to our trust in God. The more we trust in the Word and promises of God, the more we will be able to resist and deflect the temptations that the enemy shoots our way. When we raise our shield of faith, we are saying, "God, I trust you. You are for me, and not against me. The enemy's fiery darts of doubt pale in comparison to your truth." Hear this, believer: No matter how hot and no matter how many, the flaming arrows of the enemy don't stand a chance in the face of unwavering faith in Jesus Christ.

Peace is our confidence. Faith is our shield. A confidently raised shield quenches every flame that the enemy shoots our way. Lift it up! Raise that shield. Armor up. It is time we assume our victorious position in this fight. Peace and faith are ours in Jesus' name. Stand firm today, believer. God has given you all that you need to win this battle. Be the overcomer that He has made you to be!

WEEK TEN

DAY 2
TIME FOR REFLECTION

1. I love the imagery that the "gospel of peace" provides for us. Our profession of faith in Jesus puts us at peace with God. He is now for us. This is the Good News. This is the Gospel. Read Romans 5:6-10. How does this passage also reflect the truth that in Christ, God is for us?

2. Since you're already in Romans, flip over a few pages to Romans 8:31 and 8:37-39 and write out these verses below.

3. Sincere trust in God and in His Word serves as our shield of faith. According to Proverbs 30:5, what benefit do we receive when we take refuge in Him?

4. There are times when temptation seems impossible to overcome, and we can find ourselves becoming discouraged by our failure. This is precisely why it is so important for us to know the truth of God's Word. Read 1 Corinthians 10:13. What promise are we given in this verse?

DAY 3
THE ASSURANCE OF SALVATION

 "...and take the helmet of salvation..." EPHESIANS 6:17A

When I was a child, I had a nightly routine. Put on my pajamas, brush my teeth, get tucked in, say my prayers, turn on the night-light, and go to sleep. Sound familiar? One part of my regular routine that went on for years, though, might surprise you. Every night after my mom would pray for me, tell me that she loved me, and say goodnight, I would say my own prayer. It went something like this:

"God, please forgive me of all my sins today and come into my heart to be my Lord and Savior. In Jesus' name, Amen."

Although it might sound like a sweet prayer from a little child, there was much fear wrapped up into those few words. Every single night I asked God to come into my heart, again and again, because I thought that somehow, something I'd done that day had caused Him to leave. I feared losing my salvation, and I wrestled with this fear throughout much of my childhood and into adolescence. Did the sins I committed each day cause Jesus to love and forgive me any less? Thoughts of "If I die before I wake" regularly filled my little mind, always causing me to wonder, "Am I really saved?"

I genuinely wrestled with these questions when I was a child, and I can't help but wonder how many of us still toss and turn at night over these very thoughts. "Am I really saved? Will I really make it into heaven someday? Is my eternity really secure?" Friends, allow me to welcome you to the helmet of salvation. I'm so glad you're here.

So far, we've looked at the belt of truth, the breastplate of righteousness, the shoes of peace, and the shield of faith. The helmet of salvation is the next piece of armor that we're going to study. This was the piece that protected the head of the soldier, which was a constant target in battle. It's important to remember who Paul's audience is here—believers. Therefore, he is not addressing the need for salvation, but rather the assurance of salvation.

One of Satan's most frequent schemes or "flaming darts" that he shoots our way is doubt. If he can get us to doubt our salvation, we'll more than likely stop living as those who have been saved and redeemed. If he can get us to doubt our identity in Christ, he can get us to doubt Christ Himself. The more he gets us tangled up in doubt and in his web of lies, the less effective we will be in God's Kingdom here on earth. Do you see the significance of this? The enemy knows he doesn't necessarily need to win us back to his side. All he needs to do is to get us to dwell in doubt and discouragement, because when we do, our confidence disappears, and our lives become ineffective. We talked about this very thing in yesterday's lesson. The gospel of peace is our confidence, but when we begin to doubt what God's grace has done in and through us, we sideline our faith. God is inviting us back into the game today!

The battle rages on. The war isn't over yet, but the outcome has already been determined. Jesus wins. In Him, we are victorious. The confidence we need to daily stand firm in the face of this spiritual opposition is clinging to this truth:

If we are in Christ, we have been rescued from sin and death by the grace of God, and we have been given an eternal inheritance, one that not even the powers of hell can snatch from our hands. This is our confidence. The helmet of salvation is our hope of glory. We stand secure in Christ, and no scheme of the enemy could ever take that away.

WEEK TEN

DAY 3
TIME FOR REFLECTION

1. As elementary as this might sound, salvation is a free gift. When we forget this foundational truth, we get caught up in trying to earn it and deserve it. Since we can't purchase it, it's also important for us to realize that we also cannot sustain it. That is Christ's job. Read Romans 6:23 and write it out below.

2. How I would have loved to have memorized Romans 8:37-39 and understood it when I was a child. In Christ, nothing can separate us from His love. Nothing. Revisit this passage from yesterday and make a list of everything mentioned in these verses that is incapable of separating us from God's love.

3. Doubt is a seed that the enemy plants. Assurance of salvation is ours in Christ! Read each of the verses listed below and list one truth from each that speaks to our assurance of salvation.

    - John 6:37-39

    - John 10:28-29

    - Romans 5:10

    - Philippians 1:6

    - 1 Peter 1:3-5

DAY 4
PRAYING GOD'S WORD

 "...and the sword of the Spirit, which is the Word of God, praying at all times in the Spirit, with all prayer and supplication. To that end keep alert with all perseverance, making supplication for all the saints..." EPHESIANS 6:17B-18

These two verses that we're going to study today are among my favorite in the entire book of Ephesians. Have I made that claim before? Well, I think it's safe to say at this point that I have fallen head over heels in love with Paul's words to the church in Ephesus. I never knew how much one book in Scripture could mark me and capture my heart, but this one certainly has, and these two short verses have become verses that I live by. These two verses have entirely changed my approach to prayer. These two verses have gotten me on my knees more times than I can count. These two verses have shaped my faith.

This week in our study of the armor of God, we have learned that God has equipped us to be victorious in this spiritual battle by giving us these pieces of spiritual armor to protect ourselves: the belt, the breastplate, shoes, the shield, and the helmet. The common denominator that these pieces share is that they all serve as a safeguard for the soldier from the attacks of the enemy. They are all defensive in nature. Here in Ephesians 6:17-18, we are finally given two offensive pieces, weapons to fight with in this battle. Perhaps, there is only one that seems to stand out to you in our passage today. Take a closer look. We all probably take notice of the sword of the Spirit, which is the Word of God, but what is the second weapon that we are given?

Prayer.

It was a few years ago, when I first learned of the powerful and effective combination of praying God's Word—infusing Scripture into my prayers and praying God's Word right back to Him. I knew there was power in the Word, and I knew there was power in prayer. I had never thought to combine them together, though.

When we pray God's Word over our situation, it is like lighting a stick of dynamite and throwing it at our enemy. It's a force he simply cannot withstand. Whatever power the enemy has, it doesn't stand a chance against God's Word.

Take a moment to read 2 Corinthians 10:3-5 right now. How does verse four describe the weapons that we have been given?

What I find to be so interesting about this passage in 2 Corinthians is that it is a cross-reference for Ephesians 6:17-18, meaning that the weapons (plural) that are mentioned in 2 Corinthians 10 are the same weapons that we read of in Ephesians 6:17-18: God's Word and prayer. Both have tremendous power, but when we couple them together, strongholds are demolished. Chains are broken. Prisoners are set free. The enemy is defeated. We are victorious.

I have walked with the Lord for too long now to sit back, content in my own freedom while far too many remain bound. Hear the truth of God's Word spoken over you, today:

Your Heavenly Father goes before you in battle, and He is your rear guard. Jesus conquered sin and death, and He has positioned you on the victorious side with Him. Christ has clothed you with armor to protect you in this war for souls. He has given you a mighty weapon, a sword, which is His Word, and He has commanded you to use it and to persevere in prayer. Lift your sword and raise your voice. Know the Word and wield your sword! Declare the power of God's Word over the battle that rages in your life today. Get on your knees and pray. This is where our strength is found. Lean into the power of Christ. Be strong in the Lord and in the strength of His might. Put on your armor and pray God's Word.

WEEK TEN

DAY 4
TIME FOR REFLECTION

1. I love the imagery of God's Word being a sword, and Ephesians 6 is not the only place in Scripture that uses this description. Read Hebrews 4:12 and write it out below. What does "the Word of God is living and active" mean?

2. When God's Word is understood and correctly proclaimed, it has the power to demolish strongholds (2 Corinthians 10:4). A stronghold can manifest itself in our lives in a number of different ways: pride, unbelief, fear, addiction, unforgiveness, idolatry, depression, deception, insecurity, guilt, shame, and anything else that would seek to master us other than Jesus Christ. A stronghold will cause you to feel overpowered and controlled. Is there a stronghold in your life from which Christ wants to set you free?

3. Ephesians 6:18 really emphasizes the importance of prayer. In this one verse, we are instructed to pray about all things, to pray frequently, and to persevere in prayer. I can't help but wonder how many of you have grown discouraged in your prayer life. Maybe you have been praying for something for years, and you remain in a place of waiting on the Lord. What or whom have you been praying for? What verse can you choose to infuse into that prayer today? How can you begin to pray God's Word over this situation?

DAY 5
A BOLD PROCLAMATION

 "...and also for me, that words may be given to me in opening my mouth boldly to proclaim the mystery of the gospel, for which I am an ambassador in chains, that I may declare it boldly, as I ought to speak." EPHESIANS 6:19-20

Friends, we have come to our final day of homework, our last portion of Scripture in the book of Ephesians before our final lesson together, and I am simply overwhelmed with gratitude. I will be forever changed by this journey we have taken together. In-depth Bible study is no joke. When God's Word goes forth, it never returns void! I hardly ever have any idea what I'm in for when I sign up for this, but without fail, I emerge a changed woman every time. This has required commitment, dedication, determination, discipline, and steadfastness on your part. Well done.

If you are reading these words, you have made it to the end. You have run the race. You have come to the finish line. Thank you for running with me. Thank you for not giving up. I have prayed for you every day. I have envisioned your faces as you've pored over every word. I have asked the Lord to meet with you on the pages of His Word. I have believed the Lord for changed lives. I have prayed big, bold prayers. I have asked the Lord to raise up women who know and believe His Word and who live it out. I pray you are one.

If there is one thing we have learned through our study of Ephesians, I hope it's this:

Know God's Word and live God's Word—no matter the cost. Believe truth and live truth. Walk the walk. Live lives that represent Christ well—no matter the cost.

As Paul prepares to close his letter to this church that he loves so much, notice that he doesn't ask them to pray for his welfare. He is in prison. He is in chains. He has very tangible needs. The Ephesians know this, and how could Paul forget it? However, his prayer request is not for his own well-being. No. Instead, he asks them to pray that he would be bold and remain faithful in proclaiming the message of the Gospel to any and all who still need to hear it, no matter the cost. His life is of no value to himself. His one goal and his highest aim is a bold proclamation of the name of Jesus Christ and the salvation that is found in Him alone.

Could the same be said of us? Do we boldly proclaim the mystery of the Gospel? Do we even understand what is at stake? Heaven rejoices when even one sinner comes to repentance. Do we? In this battle for souls, are we a voice above the crowd shouting the message of hope? Every day we are given is another opportunity to boldly proclaim. Time is short, and the harvest is plentiful. I cannot speak for you, but I for one will not keep silent. I will not be ashamed. I will boldly proclaim the Gospel, no matter the cost.

Christ alone, the hope of all mankind, friend of sinners, Savior, Redeemer. There is no other name by which we are saved. I will boldly proclaim His name. Join me as we shout in unison,

"Awake, O sleeper, and arise from the dead, and Christ will shine on you."

"AWAKE, O SLEEPER, AND ARISE FROM THE DEAD, AND CHRIST WILL SHINE ON YOU."

WEEK TEN

DAY 5
TIME FOR REFLECTION

1. If there was ever anyone who understood the weight of his calling, it was Paul. Even unto a torturous death, Paul boldly proclaimed the mystery of the Gospel. He was an ambassador for Christ, just as we are called to be. Read 2 Corinthians 5:20 and write it out below.

2. Although we do not undergo severe religious persecution in America, we tend to bend and break under far less pressure. We fear rejection, so we keep our mouths shut. We worry about what others will think of us, so we don't boldly proclaim. According to Romans 1:16, what mindset does Paul model for us?

3. Hebrews 3:15 tells us that if you hear God's voice speaking to you today, don't harden your heart. Is God bringing anyone to mind? Is there someone in your life who needs to hear the hope of the Gospel? To whom can you boldly proclaim Jesus Christ?

4. We have come to the end of our time in Ephesians. What has God most impressed upon your heart? What lessons learned throughout this journey will mark you forever? How have you grown? In what ways have you changed?

week eleven
TO FINISH WELL WITH LOVE INCORRUPTIBLE

TEACHING OUTLINE

WEEK 11
TO FINISH WELL WITH LOVE INCORRUPTIBLE

EPHESIANS 6:21-24

- About Tychicus (verse 21)

- About Paul (verse 22)

1. All who love the Lord Jesus Christ have the assurance of _____, _____, _____, and _____. (verse 23)

2. May we _____ _____ with _____ _____. (verse 24)

 If you have committed to write out the book of Ephesians, take a few minutes right now to write Ephesians 6:21-24 in the back of your workbook.

TEACHING ANSWER KEY

WEEK 1 .... Page 11
1. hardest heart; softened
2. faithful; faithless
3. grace; peace

WEEK 2 .... Page 23
1. Wanted
2. Highly regarded
3. Overcomers

WEEK 3 .... Page 37
1. result
2. hope
3. leads; assurance

WEEK 4 .... Page 49
1. reminder; redeemed
2. world
3. enemy
4. children of wrath

WEEK 5 .... Page 61
1. desire; lost
2. love; preferences
3. understood; embraced; withhold
4. rules; Jesus; projects; religion

WEEK 6 .... Page 75
1. Submission; reverence; define
2. spiritual strength
3. prayers; reflection

WEEK 7 .... Page 87
1. futility; ignorance; callousness; impurity
2. knowledge; responsibility
3. head; heart; behavior

WEEK 8 .... Page 99
1. love
2. love; obey
3. go, went; do, did; love, loved

WEEK 9 .... Page 115
1. obedience
2. policy; protection
3. Submission is not…
4. attitude; cooperation; choice

WEEK 10 .... Page 127
1. frighten; prepare
2. Enemy; enemy
3. enables; stand firm; wavering

WEEK 11 .... Page 143
1. peace, love, faith, grace
2. finish well; love incorruptible

EPHESIANS 1

EPHESIANS 2

EPHESIANS 3

EPHESIANS 4

AWAKE O SLEEPER

EPHESIANS 5

EPHESIANS 6

Made in the USA
Columbia, SC
17 November 2023